NO LAST WORDS

TARA KELLY

NO LAST WORDS

A MEMOIR OF MARRIAGE

EASTOVER
— PRESS —

For McCullough and Jack

Love? I thought you'd never ask. My friend,
love is a hard master and a poor servant,
but only a slightly difficult friend.

Can I still change my tune? Well,
you may wonder; but would you
notice is what I can't tell.

from "Ars Brevis: Primavera," a sonnet
by Brian C. Kelly

NO LAST WORDS

WEDDING TOASTS

NEW YORK CITY—OCTOBER 1988

"You know they're taking bets at the bar that you guys won't last a year," Scott told me. I laughed, though I didn't think it was funny.

"I hope you haven't bet against us," I said.

Scott was a friend of Robert's from 211, the restaurant and bar in Tribeca where we met. He was a painter. A Vietnam vet. Someone whose own dating history revolved around unattainable romantic ideals. He didn't admit to it, but I assumed he'd placed the first wager. His toast at our wedding reception mentioned the bet.

Haywood, Robert's best man, stood up to make his toast. Haywood was, and is, kind, gentle, soft-spoken. He and his longtime girlfriend, Vicki, spent so much time with Robert and his first wife, Colby, that Haywood was fretting he would say the wrong name when it came time to toast Robert and me. No one remembers what words of good cheer, what forecasts for our rosy future Haywood bestowed on us, because when he asked our friends and family to raise a glass to Robert and Tara, despite his being soft-spoken, there was not a person in the room who didn't hear him when he said, "To Robert and Colby."

Poor Haywood. I wasn't jealous of Robert's past, but that didn't mean I wanted his ex-wife making a nominal appearance at my wedding. Still, I could recognize the cinematic nature of the moment. Haywood sat down. Miserable. He apologized profusely to me when we danced, as he stepped all over my cream-colored satin shoes, which I minded much more than the bungled toast.

Then my brother Brian stood up. I'd seen him earlier, sitting at the bar scribbling on tiny pages of white note paper:

> Remember the beetles we dropped into the jars of
>   gasoline—saving the potatoes?
> While we worked, a very white bird circled over the field.
> There are birds like that in fairy tales and there is one
>   now, for real.
> I thought that bird was you. I still see that bird when
>   you smile.
> Life doesn't get sharper than the moments you perceive
>   as poetry.
> Love can be poetry. The memory of childhood moments
>   can be poetry.
> The most remarkable accomplishment is confidence in
>   the poetry of your own future.

My brother said, "Love can be poetry." It was something to aspire to, but Robert and I never achieved it. Our love was prosaic, and fraught. We had lived our marriage vows, ticking off the boxes—"for better, for worse, for richer, for poorer, in sickness, in health, to love and cherish"— except that last part, "to cherish." *Cherish*. It's an old-fashioned word that conveys devotion and a depth of feeling. It suggests intimacy and true caring. I knew I had loved and cherished Robert, but I honestly didn't know if he had cherished me.

Right up to his death I never really knew where I stood with him. It seemed to me he was always standing in the way of us. What were we to each other? I've spent the past decade trying to answer that question for myself.

NO LAST WORDS

WEDNESDAY, JUNE 27, 2012
LAKEVILLE, CONNECTICUT

The day before Robert died was an otherwise perfect June day in Connecticut: warm but not hot, with a bit of a breeze, flawless blue sky, puffy white clouds—the sort of weather a sailor loves, and Robert was a sailor. I opened the French doors in my bedroom so he would have a greater sense of the outside world. If he noticed, he made no comment. He didn't seem to be aware of the weather.

He was settled in among the many pillows on my king-size bed, wearing one of his black T-shirts and a robe. The bed was a problem, as it was high off the ground and he had to climb up into it, which was difficult because of the pain in his abdomen. There was a mango-sized lump just below his rib cage. His liver was engorged with tumors. Robert, a man accustomed to barreling through the world in a fast car or a fast boat, sometimes carrying me along in his slipstream, sometimes leaving me behind, now needed a stepstool and my steady hand to make it easier for him to climb slowly, carefully into the bed. I hovered at his elbow so he could lean on me.

He was slipping in and out of lucidity. I sat next to him, close enough to touch, but on top of the covers, with my computer on my lap catching up on email. We shared the bed as though this day was just another of the many we'd spent together.

His friends, our families were checking in. Could they drop by? Should they come? My sisters Sarah and Ursula called. They were meeting up in Boston and driving out. I reminded Robert that his lawyer, Skip Rodgers, was scheduled to stop by at one o'clock with papers for him to sign: a power of attorney for me, and Robert's new will.

On our honeymoon, sitting on the veranda of the pink stucco hotel on the beach in Bermuda with the remains of a room-service breakfast still on the table before us, Robert suddenly jumped up. "I need to make a call," he said. Using the room phone, he dialed the States. "I have to talk to my lawyer," he said by way of explanation. I pretended to be absorbed in the *New York Times,* as though if I were reading I would not overhear his conversation.

When his lawyer was finally on the line, he told him he'd gotten remarried.

"Just three days ago. —Thank you. —We're in Bermuda. —Just for a few days; Tara has to get back to work. —Right. She needs to be in my will, and obviously, remove Colby." He spelled out my full name. I was glad the paper was hiding my face. I thought I should be as matter-of-fact as Robert was, and I didn't trust myself to disguise that his call had thrilled me. This was the moment I felt truly married.

Almost twenty-four years later, the will was relevant again. He was dying. We didn't know how long he had to live, but Robert was hastily putting his affairs in order. The power of attorney was for me in the event he lost lucidity and couldn't manage his business. But the will itself would be very simple: he was leaving everything to our children, McCullough and Jack. I was pretty sure I wasn't in it. I was no longer his wife. Robert and I were divorced. So I was—what?

I was the one who stepped up to the big requests, who helped him open a restaurant, not once but twice. The second time with loathing and dread, knowing what I was in for. I was the one who withstood the myriad little indignities and the larger emotional assaults brought on by years of alcoholism. Who endured the cycles of on and off the wagon. Who said, "I can't be married to you if you're going to drink." And who then suffered the brunt of his anger even after he relented and went to rehab. I was the one who put the photo album together with the pictures of the good times, the friends, his children, and his family, who all wanted him to get better—and the one who drove the five hours to Caron Family Center because alcoholism is a family disease, and you have to treat the whole family for the alcoholic to have a chance of not drinking.

I was the one who believed in the kind and considerate Robert. I kept my faith with him, even though he didn't show up very often. I was the one who'd said, just twenty-three days before, when he got the diagnosis of liver cancer, "Of course, you'll come home whenever you want."

Robert lay dozing in bed next to me. We were alone in the room. I wondered if I should be asking him questions. Getting him to talk about what was on his mind. Was he worried about dying? It didn't seem so. Early on Robert had said, "I don't want to die. But I'm not going to fight this thing. I'm not going to go to every doctor I can find looking for a cure. I don't want to spend my last days in a hospital."

He said that he wanted to show McCullough and Jack that there was nothing to be afraid of. I wondered if he still felt that way. Was he afraid now? Should I ask him if there was anything he particularly wanted me to do? Should we be talking about funeral arrangements? Songs? Hymns? Readings? My mother is constantly updating me on her thoughts about her funeral service and burial plans. A lapsed Catholic, drawn to Buddhism, she's settled on the Unitarian Universalist church in Wellesley, Massachusetts, where she lives. She feels the need for ceremony, ritual, a celebration of life. But that's my mother.

Neither Robert nor I were religious. We never went to church. We got married in his loft in Tribeca in New York City. There would be no priest or last rites, but still, I thought, shouldn't we be talking about this, talking today about his dying?

Suddenly Robert murmured, "Slow down for that curve ahead," and I imagined he was back in his race car, perhaps negotiating the track at Lime Rock. Both hands on the wheel, at ten and at two, eyes fixed intently on the road in front of him. The way he always drove, even just around town. We could pass each other on the road, and he would never wave, the way others did, recognizing each other by their car, so involved was he when he was driving.

One of the reasons we'd moved to Lakeville was the proximity of Lime Rock Park, a favorite racetrack of his. Robert had always loved cars, had owned dozens, and particularly loved to race. For years it was a series of Honda CRXs. Then he joined the Sports Car Club of America and converted an Alfa Romeo for the track. He'd had a Lola that we trailered to Savannah, Georgia, for a week of racing. It was the one time I went along, hung out at the track with him, played the part of a pit crew member.

Robert was fully engaged when he was behind the wheel of a car. He'd perfected the heel/toe shift that racers use. His left foot positioned above the clutch, his right foot dancing back and forth from gas pedal to brake. His eyes sweeping from sideview mirror to rearview mirror to sideview and back again. He could feel the motor and its rhythms with his whole body. The feel of the car as the RPMs rose, letting him know when it was time to shift. Clutch, shift, gas. A renewed burst of speed. He drove with total concentration, but it was effortless.

Effortless—the way he wielded a knife in the kitchen, at home or in his restaurant. Fingers curled back out of the way of the knife blade—a whole carrot or onion separating into identically sized slices as the knife moved rhythmically down the chopping board. Then he'd pivot on his heel and scrape the slices into the pot on the stove. With a flick of his wrist, he'd shake the sauté pan, press the meat with his thumb to check its doneness, and sprinkle a liberal pinch of kosher salt over whatever he was cooking. His fluidity of motion made it seem he did all five things at once.

Effortless—the way he piloted a boat. The way he navigated the waters of Somes Sound and the Western Way. At the helm of *Raven,* he would swing her around to tie up at the float off Greenings. The force of the tide there off the northwestern tip of the island made it tricky, but Robert—playing the throttle, gunning the engine just enough—would bring her starboard side smoothly along the dock. He would throw the gear into neutral and nimbly hop off, lines in hand, three times around the cleat, and one loop to knot it. He would secure the boat while his passengers would still be asking, "Can I help?"

There would be no more driving, no more cooking, no more boating. When Dr. Kruger had told him that a few days before, it was the first time since the diagnosis I'd seen Robert get upset. It was perhaps the first time that the magnitude of what was happening to Robert's body became real for either of us. I thought of everything I knew about cancer and its treatment from friends who had died and friends who had survived. I'd seen them go through difficult regimens of chemo and radiation that resulted in nausea, vomiting, hair loss, extreme fatigue. I thought of all the things we would need to do to get through it, the adjustments that would be made, the transformation of the bedroom into a sickroom. I reviewed the possible scenarios and different outcomes.

After my friend Cletus died, I'd read two books on death and dying. Sherwin Nuland's *How We Die* and Elisabeth Kübler-Ross's *On Death and Dying.* At the time I was looking for some kind of guide to the transformative experience of death. Nuland's book sounded promising by its subtitle, *Reflections on Life's Final Chapter.* It was not, it turned out, a primer for a "good" death or a meaningful exit; rather, it was a blow-by-blow description of how the body deteriorates as it succumbs to a variety of different diseases. In thorough and often excruciating detail, Nuland describes death by heart disease, by Alzheimer's, by cancer, even by murder. Death can be a violent and messy business as the body insistently holds on, overriding heart and mind and soul to cling to life.

From this book I had a sense of what any of us might expect. It seemed that Cletus, though she must have been in a lot of pain, and certainly was discomfited by the treatments to cure her, had gotten off lightly. Nuland writes in the introduction: "The quest to achieve true dignity fails when our bodies fail. Occasionally—very occasionally— unique circumstances of death will be granted to someone with a unique personality, and that lucky combination will make it happen, but such a confluence of fortune is uncommon, and, in any case, not to be expected by any but a very few people." I had no expectation that Robert would be lucky, unique, or one of the very few.

From Nuland I knew to expect a tough passage. Kübler-Ross offered the five stages of death that had become the accepted route for dying—so much so that one was expected to go through denial, anger, bargaining, depression, and acceptance, and in that order. If a person did not, then it was probably evidence that they were stuck on Step One, denial. It seemed that Robert had gone right to acceptance. As usual, disregarding the norms.

But true to form I was going to help him do it right. That morning I'd called a friend and asked her to meet me at the office of the Salisbury Visiting Nurse Association. She and I were on the ambulance squad together, we'd gone on a nursing mission to the Dominican Republic with my sister Ursula, we rode our horses and walked our dogs together, but I'd been away at school and I'd hardly had a chance to update her on Robert's condition.

Sitting in the hospice director's office reviewing end-of-life decisions and what Robert would need felt wrong and premature, because it still didn't seem like he was dying. Robert hadn't even been on the chemo pills long enough for them to make him ill, much less have an effect on the cancer. Now we were talking about hospital beds and morphine and ways to make him comfortable. He's perfectly comfortable, I thought.

He's in a nice bed in a nice room with his friends arriving for a visit. A hospital bed would take up all the floor space. It would be antiseptic.

It would be a statement: he's dying.

"It will make it easier to care for him," the hospice director said. "Easier for him to get in and out of; you can raise the head or the foot as desired. If he becomes incontinent, it won't stain your bed," she said.

"I guess I don't really want him to die in my bed," I finally admitted. They said it could be delivered that afternoon. A hospice nurse would stop by and introduce herself and get a baseline on Robert.

"Yes, okay," but I explained that Ursula, who was a nurse, and her girlfriend Kathy, also a nurse, would be there by late afternoon, and they would take care of him and administer any drugs that he needed.

"Do you want a social worker to come by and talk with the family?"

"Hardly necessary," I said.

"Well, when it gets closer to the time, let us know if you change your mind."

When I returned to the house, my mother, Therese, was in the kitchen making lunch and fielding phone calls. Jack was upstairs sorting out his camping and rock-climbing gear. McCullough wasn't home yet. I was anxious for her to arrive. Therese ran through a list of people who had checked in: Haywood and John called from the road; they expected to be here by four. My brothers, Brian and Justin, were planning to drive up from the city that night. Robert's sister Barbara would arrive on the weekend.

Earlier one of the waitstaff from his restaurant had dropped off a chocolate milkshake. "It's the one thing I know he loves," she said. It stood untouched by the bedside except for a sip when she brought it. Robert wasn't hungry.

I settled in again next to him on the bed. Robert's friend Brendan walked into the room. My bedroom is on the first floor at the end of a long hallway, but an easy distance to the living room, kitchen, and front door. When Brendan came in, Robert woke up and greeted him with a big smile. They talked for a few minutes; Brendan wrapped it up with, "I love you, man." I walked Brendan to the front door.

"What's going on? How is he?" Brendan asked.

"I don't know. A few days ago, it seemed like he was losing lucidity. Now, it's more like he's just sleeping a lot. Dr. Kruger told us two to three weeks."

"Okay if I check in later?" Brendan asked.

"Of course, and will you let others know they can stop by to see him?"

It was finally registering with me that Robert was dying. And yet I still couldn't see it happening. Even as I wrote emails to friends suggesting they come by and visit, even as I said he's losing lucidity, even as his dozing turned more into a deep sleep, I couldn't fathom that the end was so near. I was saying it, but I wasn't believing it. I was doing everything I could think of to take care of Robert and fulfill desires he wasn't expressing. He wasn't giving me any guidance. He didn't want anything anymore.

Within an hour his friends, our friends, started showing up. Some of them had come to say goodbye. Others came thinking they were just checking in. Each time someone new walked into the room, Robert brightened. If he was dozing, he woke up. Everyone was greeted with a big hello and a smile. A half a minute, a few words, and he'd start to fade again.

There was a moment around nine in the evening when Robert came to life. He hadn't gotten out of bed all day. He hadn't had anything to eat or drink. The hospital bed had been delivered and set up. We all negotiated our way around it as my room is not large and the two beds together took up most of the floor space.

"Should we move him?" I'd asked Ursula after the bed arrived.

"We can wait until he needs to get up," she said.

That happened at nine. Robert wasn't coherent or steady on his feet, but he wanted to go to the bathroom. By himself. Ursula tried to get him to use a bedpan. No. He wouldn't. And suddenly he was thrashing. Insistent and irritable, but not sensible.

"Brian can go with him," I said. It seemed such a small thing to let him walk the twenty feet to the bathroom and back if that's what he wanted.

Ursula, who had been a nurse to AIDS patients, knew what was happening: the liver was no longer working, the toxins were building up, and his brain was being poisoned. She knew that Robert's body was shutting down. But for me, irritable Robert was familiar. This was the most animated he'd been all day. And he *wanted* something. And I wanted him to have it. Even if it was just a trip to the bathroom. This is what I was prepared for. I could not see the end in sight.

LUCKY

MAINE 1951

Robert was lucky. It seemed to most everyone who knew him that Robert had been dealt a winning hand. He seemed to absorb luck—turning the bad kind around, making the most of the good kind. The circumstances of his birth. He was the child of an unwed mother. Not so promising, maybe. Then he won the lottery when he was adopted into a wealthy family. But four years later he was diagnosed with kidney cancer. His adoptive mother drew on her considerable resources and connections, and he survived.

Luck or a bad oyster spared his life when he was in his late twenties. Robert and his first wife, Colby, had gone to New Orleans for the weekend. A lovely hotel in the French Quarter. Bottles of rosé champagne to drink while eating heaps of chilled crayfish the same color as the wine. And oysters. Robert loved oysters. He always said it was a bad one that left him too sick to get on the flight home. The flight that crashed shortly after takeoff, killing all on board. He was matter-of-fact when he told me the story. If he was affected by the enormity of what he'd escaped, he didn't say so. There was plenty of evidence that Robert lived with luck on his side. But he wore it lightly. Years later he took me to New Orleans for the weekend. We stayed in the same hotel, ate in the same restaurants. We went because he loved New Orleans, the romance of it, the way it fit loosely around you, the vibe that said, feeling good is what life is all about. Robert lived in the moment, or in a borrowed future. He never dwelt on the past.

Robert Willis wasn't born with that name. It was the name his parents gave him when they collected him at four months old from the Home for Little Wanderers in Boston. In November 1951, Jim and Martha Willis drove from Southwest Harbor, Maine, to Boston to collect the infant boy they would name Robert. The seven-plus-hour drive along the coast of Maine took them through small seaside villages—Belfast, Camden, Rockland, Wiscasset, Bath. His biological parents were from one of those towns, or one very much like them.

When Robert was adopted, the director of the agency gave Jim and Martha a one-page typed document that told his story. It didn't name names or give details that would reveal identities; it said:

> The mother was twenty-one years old. The father was
> twenty-seven.

The mother and father are from the same town and grew up together. They were in love with each other and were to be married in August, but his mother broke up the marriage. The father is stationed away but has been back to see the mother. The father is a major in the Army soon to be a colonel. He is an expert in radar and electronics.

The mother was the youngest child in a big family. She was the family favorite. All of them graduated from high school. They are all upright, intelligent, industrious, thoroughly respected citizens. There are no "black sheep." They have a tendency to good voices, and to play the piano. Her older married sister wanted to take the baby, but they couldn't figure out how to explain it.

It was decided that the mother would go to Boston to have the baby and give it up for adoption. Everyone was told that she got a "position out of town." She came back after the baby was delivered. The document went on to describe both parents as being from Anglo-Scottish stock. The father had prematurely gray hair and was six feet tall. He had good teeth and a strong heart. Then it describes the baby:

> He is a very good baby. Not fussy. Is affectionate and likes to be held. Is timid of strangers, loud noises,

and sudden movements. He is big for his age and is
considered by the agency doctor to be unusually bright.
He is a homely baby, well-shaped head, high forehead,
gray-blue eyes, perfect skin, flat ears.

From the moment Robert told me the story of his birth I was transfixed by its inherent drama. He could be living in the very same town as his birth parents. They might have gotten married after giving him up. Maybe he had brothers and sisters living in a town that we passed through every summer on our way to and from Mount Desert Island. Maybe one day we would encounter the six-foot-tall man with prematurely gray hair, good teeth, and a strong heart. The description covered his physical attributes, but for the rest you had to read between the lines. Strong heart but not strong character, at least not enough to stand up to his mother, marry his sweetheart, and become a father to his son.

Robert wasn't interested in speculating.

"I never really think about it, Tara," he said. I knew that wasn't true. He was the one who told me, unprompted, about the story behind his adoption, and he wasn't unaware of its entertainment value. He kept the letter from the adoption home in a box in his bedroom. I suspect he didn't want to look for his birth parents. "What if they were needy or wanted something from me?" That's not a direct quote, but I remember him saying something like that. While there are plenty of wealthy communities up and down the coast, most of the inhabitants are working-class tradespeople and fishermen. I think Robert didn't want anything to disturb his comfortable perch.

Robert was willing enough to spin the tale, but he was never forthcoming with his feelings about it. And that was true about so many of our conversations. Robert could tell me the name and the year of a wine he had at a dinner when he was sixteen in Paris, but he couldn't tell me how he felt about being adopted.

He wasn't introspective. It might be that Robert didn't just not tell me: perhaps he didn't tell himself. Robert had been seeing a psychiatrist for years.

"Sometimes I go and lie on the couch and don't say anything."

"What do you mean you don't say anything?" I asked. "Doesn't the doctor ask you questions?"

"No. Sometimes I go to his office and lie down on the couch. I don't say anything, and after forty-five minutes I get up and leave."

"But that's crazy. That's such a waste."

Robert shrugged. "I'd been seeing him for more than six months before I told him I was adopted."

Robert might deny thinking about his birth family, but I thought about them often. I thought about his birth mother and the agony of giving up a child. She was engaged to be married, and her future mother-in-law broke up the engagement. Is it because she knew about the pregnancy? Or didn't they tell her? The birth mother had to have hoped that her pregnancy would raise the stakes enough that her beau would stand up to his mother and go through with the marriage. Should she have known better? When the crushing disappointment of his indifference, or inability, was made clear, she hoped that her child could at least stay in the family. There are plenty of children out there being raised by their grandmother, with an older sister who's really the mother. I mined that document from the Home for Little Wanderers for evidence of who Robert was. When he didn't stand up for himself or made decisions that I thought were an easy out, I saw in him his birth father—turning away from his girlfriend, and unborn child.

While I often overstepped the bounds of what was my business or right to comment on, I did believe that on this subject it was Robert's right to investigate or ignore. And perhaps I didn't push him, because if he were successful then I too would have to deal with another family putting demands on Robert, and I felt as though there was little enough of him on offer. It's also true that no one ever came looking for him. Not his birth mother, or father, or that aunt who wanted to adopt him herself.

And that seemed fine with him. Robert was deeply affected by the love and generosity of Gramps, his adopted grandfather on his mother's side. In a photograph from that era, a tall, angular man with a hawk nose rests his hand lightly on the shoulder of a young, slightly pudgy boy, who is standing perhaps a little taller than he ordinarily would. Robert told me:

- Gramps went to court in 1951 and spent one million dollars to successfully change the terms of a family trust that prohibited adopted children from inheriting.
- Gramps taught him how to surf on a family vacation in Hawaii.
- Gramps gave him his first gun and taught him how to shoot a .22 on a family vacation in Montana.
- The enormous boathouse on the harbor in Camden that now is home to a boat brokerage used to belong to Gramps.

This I learned one of the first times we drove together to Mount Desert Island. Following Route 1 along the coast, just as Jim and Martha Willis did when they returned from Boston with their baby boy, we stopped finally in Camden. By 1986, Camden had been completely transformed from a prosperous nineteenth-century seafaring town to a tourist destination. Nearly every grand house on the main street had been turned into a bed and breakfast or an inn, parking was at a premium, and all the restaurants, cafes, and ice cream shops were crowded with tourists on vacation.

We parked on a side street and wandered down to the water. Picturesque as the postcards you could buy in every store, the harbor was full of boats. Robert pointed out the boathouse, across the way from where we stood. It was a long, shingled building with doors opening directly onto the water. It had been built in the early 1900s to house Chauncey Borland's (Gramps) 140-foot Lawley steam yacht. Robert never stepped aboard that boat—the U.S. government requisitioned it during World War I. Though it had been decades since his grandfather died, and as many years since the boathouse was sold, Robert's attachment to the family lore was as tenacious as the barnacles that clung to the pier.

I think all those years later Robert was still impressed by his grandfather's wealth and used it to define himself. And I think he was wooing me in a nineteenth-century Jane Austen sort of way. In *Pride and Prejudice,* Mrs. Bennett repeats what she has heard about Mr. Darcy: "They say he has 10,000 a year!" The calculation and evaluation of a suitor's wealth were tied to his eligibility. Later on that same trip, as we drove around Southwest Harbor, he pointed out a house he'd bought and sold. Even though he didn't own it anymore, it was from his perspective still part of a portfolio. My reaction, which I did not share, was, "I'd be more impressed if you still owned it." I'd already gleaned that Robert's attachments were often transitory. Real estate, cars, objects—they could be status symbols, and valuable or meaningless depending on your state of mind. Was there a corollary between his desire for things and his desire for me? Robert was married when we met. Was this previously owned house representative of the ex-wife? Would I one day be replaced as she had been?

When, as a child, Robert was diagnosed with Wilms tumor, his prognosis was poor. The survival rate today is about 93 percent. In 1955, it was considerably less. Living in a small seacoast town the nearest hospitals offered only routine medical care, not the specialized cancer care he needed. His mother took him to Boston Children's Hospital, which at that time had the best care available. Robert couldn't recall all the details—he was four years old when they first went to Boston—but he remembered that his mother took a suite in one of the grander hotels facing the Commons for the weeks surrounding the surgery, and recuperation, followed by radiation treatments. There were many trips to Boston after that—trips that he loved both for the extended one-on-one time with his mother and because he loved going to the city. A place where he didn't stand out the way he did at home. His childhood was overshadowed by years of physical therapy and his parents cautioning him against hurting himself. He wasn't allowed to play sports as a boy; football was too rough and baseball too strenuous. But he could pilot a boat.

His father, Jim, had a boat-building business and sold Boston Whalers, skiffs with an outboard motor. Robert worked for his father every summer. When he was a kid, he would make money by collecting sand dollars, bleaching them in the sun, and selling them for a dollar each to the customers who came to his father's boathouse. When he was a teenager, he worked at the boatyard doing any and all jobs required of a dock boy. He washed, sanded, and varnished boats; worked as a sailing instructor and outboard mechanic; and skippered summer residents out to their yachts.

He was straddling two worlds. It was a yin-yang pull that defined and challenged him his whole life. On the one side, his mother's world of inherited wealth. It was understated and oh-so-quiet, nothing flashy or ostentatious, but she had the means to do pretty much whatever she wanted. Yet she married a man who wanted to live away from the world of her parents, and though they met in Camden, a very tony enclave of summer residents, they settled in Southwest Harbor, a two-hour drive Down East. It was populated by lobstermen and tradespeople serving the summer residents there and in the equally posh town of Northeast Harbor. Robert's mother would take him and his sister for vacations with her parents to Hawaii, Montana, and Caneel Bay on St. John's Island, a resort built in 1956 by Laurance Rockefeller, who also summered on Mount Desert.

Then he would come home to his father's stern expectation that he disregard that life of leisure and earn his respect by hard work. Jim had turned away from a life defined by how much money one had. While not as rich as his wife, his family was from Greenwich, Connecticut, itself a town synonymous with wealth. By the time I met Jim, he had retired from the boat business and was living with his second wife, Lou, in a ranch-style house he'd built himself. Robert's parents had divorced after Jim had an affair with Lou. Lou was "local." I think Robert told me she was the secretary at the boat business.

Jim would sit on a stool at the kitchen counter smoking one cigarette after another, as we all struggled to find something to talk about that didn't end after a sentence or two. Our visits were always in the summer while we were on vacation, and that itself seemed to signal to Jim that Robert didn't work hard enough. It was a lifelong struggle for Robert to earn his father's respect.

Shortly after we met, Robert invited me up to his loft. He had recently renovated it and installed a fireplace in his library. Not a usual thing to find in a loft in Tribeca. Like his father, he had done the work himself. In front of a blazing fire in a room that looked out over the Hudson River and the sparkling New York City skyline with the Empire State Building front and center, Robert told me the story of his life, tearing up as he talked about his mother. She had died less than a year before. She was the source of all good things in his life. It was clear that she was devoted to him and that he loved her unconditionally. He never said a negative thing about her or his Gramps.

Robert completely embraced the history and lifestyle of his mother's family, the Borlands. There were stories behind the monogrammed silver, the Steuben glass, and gold-plated flatware that filled the glass-fronted cabinets in his dining room. The Elie Nadelman bronze stag, the Hunt Diederich fireplace screen, the Raoul Dufy oil painting of the Eiffel Tower. Everything came with a name and a provenance. It wasn't just a fireplace screen. It was a Diederich, which his grandparents had purchased directly from the artist after a visit to his studio. His devotion to the mementos and lore of the Borlands was mythological.

In the ninth grade, Robert went away to prep school. The public high school on Mount Desert Island wasn't held in high regard, and after looking at Groton, St. Paul's, and Deerfield, Robert and his mother chose Phillips Academy Andover. Robert showed me his senior class Andover yearbook. His classmates wrote under his photo: "Robert B. Willis — Walks Like He Is." When I read that, I knew immediately what it meant. Robert had a way about him. Part-shuffle, part-glide, he walked as though he were Fred Astaire about to enter a ballroom. He had a way of smiling. A way of holding a cigarette or a glass of wine that was self-possessed but not arrogant. With his shirt on, he looked muscular and well-built. He had broad shoulders and that narrow waist—an odd cutout on his right side—so that his pants never fit quite right, and his belt rode up a bit on the right. He didn't know or remember if it was the surgery or the subsequent radiation that left his torso misshapen. He always insisted that he didn't mind about that. It was, he noted, his chin he was self-conscious about. He thought it was weak. He always wanted a chiseled chin. The adoption document didn't mention which side of his family he'd inherited that defect from. That was how Robert saw it, as a defect.

Luck is such a loaded word. When good things happen seemingly out of nowhere, we say it's good luck, but maybe behind that is intention, patience, perseverance, hard work. When bad things happen, we say, that's bad luck, but maybe behind that is carelessness, poor choices, thoughtlessness. Was Robert lucky to have been adopted into a wealthy family? Most people would say, "Yes!" But there's plenty of anecdotal evidence that inherited wealth kills the initiative to work hard and "make something of oneself." When the measure for making something of oneself is earning a lot of money and you already have a lot, then why work hard? Of course, this is not true for everyone; in fact, Robert could and did work incredibly hard but erratically, and not always to earn money—it was to fulfill dreams. But what about the complicating factor of inheriting the wealth through adoption? And something else that's inherited, the DNA for alcoholism. And maybe, considering genetics, was the Wilms tumor traceable to his birth parents, or was that just bad luck?

What do we attribute outcomes to? Is it possible that undergoing severe challenges in childhood fills the mind with a sense of life as both uncontrollable and survivable? Good luck, bad luck, a roll of the dice. Surviving becomes its own luck.

Hopefully, by the time we reach adulthood we seek self-determination. When it comes to our lives, and hopes for our future, sometimes we need to put aside the past. Robert thought his path was clearly delineated. Prep school leads to a good college, leads to a good job, with the better part of every summer spent in Maine. An expectation born of a certain lifestyle. When did Robert's path mutate away from that preordained course? With the death of his mother? With the subsequent inheritance? With the increase of his drinking? With his admission that he was an alcoholic? For the longest time, these were not questions Robert seemed to consider. When he did, when he went to rehab, the answers seemed to elude him.

AMBIVALENCE

NEW YORK CITY 1987

In the 1990s rom-com *When Harry Met Sally,* the character played by Carrie Fisher, one of Sally's best friends, is having an affair. She is continually turning up evidence that her lover is still enamored of his wife. As she confides each incident to Sally, she ends with, "I don't think he's going to leave his wife." Each time Sally answers her, "No one thinks he's ever going to leave his wife."

We often know the essential truth of our relationships even when we don't want to admit it, even to ourselves. Even when our friends point it out to us. Even in the face of clear and convincing evidence. We dedicate ourselves to proving the narrative that we prefer, the one that says that the 10 or 20 percent of the person we love is the true reflection of them, that the 80 percent that perpetually disappoints, that's the anomaly.

But the insistence of the psyche to be heard and healed isn't so easily resolved. Robert, whether either of us realized it or not, had all the makings of an unavailable man. I think some part of me recognized the signs—obscured as they were by his charm, exuberance, and willingness to share his life with me. Yet there was always an underlying disinterest in me. Robert put himself and his needs, wants, and desires first, time and again. And I accepted it, even as I objected. I took care of the kids, and the houses, and kept life running smoothly around him; I kept his dreams alive even when he had moved on to new ones.

I did this, even though early on I was introduced to the idea that my choice of Robert as my life partner might have more to do with my past than with my future. I was twenty-seven and recently engaged to Robert. I was on the verge of an exciting new life, and yet I was mired in a persistent misery. I was seeing a therapist in the hopes of straightening myself out before the wedding. A quick fix. As if it could ever be that easy.

I sat in the waiting room of my therapist's office on the Upper West Side flipping through the magazines on the coffee table. I picked up the *Atlantic Monthly* and started to read an article. It said that people choose partners with whom they can unconsciously work out their issues. So a woman whose father was remote and unavailable, for instance, might choose a man who was emotionally warm, who laughed and cried easily, thinking she was getting the opposite of what she'd grown up with. But over time, that man could be revealed to be as unavailable as the father had been. Was he that way from the beginning and she just didn't see it? Or was her unconscious need to relive the past, to find the familiar, so strong she would turn him into the distant father? It was a disturbing thought.

I brought the magazine into the session with me.

"Is this true?" I showed the article to the therapist.

"It can be."

"You mean I'm going to turn Robert into Tom? It's going to be *my* fault?"

"Well, Tara, being aware of the possibility is the first step toward changing it."

My father, Tom, was the definition of remote and unavailable. Picture a tall, slender man with a perpetually serious expression. Close-cropped hair. Wire-rimmed glasses. I see the iconic painting *American Gothic* by Grant Wood with its stolid air of menace (that pitchfork) and think of my father. The farmer dressed in overalls and a suit jacket. My father was a teacher who farmed to feed his family. My parents' embrace of parenthood was reluctant at best. For starters, we always called them by their first names. No Mom and Dad for them.

My parents separated when I was twelve, and after that I only saw Tom for a couple of weeks in the summers. As my brothers and sisters and I became teenagers and took on summer jobs, our visits to him stopped. Even though my grandfather, his father, had taken in my mother and the six of us, Tom didn't come to see us at Thanksgiving or Christmas. He didn't write letters or send cards. He didn't call.

He didn't like talking on the phone. He didn't much like talking. He existed in a self-imposed shroud of silence.

He was a college professor. I never heard him teach, and I tried to picture how a man who didn't like to talk could stand in a lecture hall, in front of a hundred or so students, and speak at length. He wrote his thesis on Edgar Allan Poe. Would he have discussed with his students the story he liked to tell us when we were children? The one about the lady who always wore a black velvet choker around her neck. Her lover questioned her as to why and pestered her endlessly to remove it. Finally, she relented and untied the ribbon. Her head fell off. At least, that's how I remember Tom telling the story.

Our summer visits reinforced for me how grim life would have been if we'd moved with him to upstate New York. Actually, the visits reinforced how grim life had been in the years we did live with him. Tom didn't seem to know what to do with us, except put us to work. He'd bought a small farmhouse. Like all the houses we lived in it was this side of ramshackle. The first summer we spent our days helping him reshingle it. When we were exhausted by the sun and the precision required to place the shingles with just the right amount of overlap, we took refuge inside and watched the Watergate hearings. I was entranced by Maureen Dean, her white earrings, her high-necked cream-colored dress, her white-blonde hair pulled into a tight bun. She was a blank slate, an icon of contained composure. I'd never seen a woman like her. Her husband, John, in horn-rimmed glasses and a Brooks Brothers suit, was an intellectual on trial, explaining away his misdeeds. They were so upright and correct. They didn't seem to notice that they'd blurred the lines between right and wrong. From my seat in front of the TV, I saw my father in the kitchen with my Aunt Mary, his brother's wife; she was sharing the house with him. His hand traversed her back and rested on her bottom.

I took the magazine with me when I left the therapist's office and thought about it often. The article seemed to be a crystal ball into my marriage. These sentences described the dynamic of our relationship: "She had created a space for him at the very center of her life and was now in a state of some dependency—increasingly reliant upon him in terms of the outcome of her own fate, and therefore ever more committed to remaining blind to certain signals that he might not be as wonderfully nurturing a person as she initially believed him to be."

Yet I was not as blind as the sample woman in the article. While I had turned my fate over to Robert, it was not without constant chafing and reassessment. Over the years I was less and less enthralled, yet still enmeshed. My need for Robert to be who I wanted him to be trumped every indication that he wasn't. I chose any shred of evidence that he loved, valued, and respected me, over evidence that he did not. Maybe it wasn't that he didn't love, value, and respect me, it's that he did it to the best of his ability and that fell far short of my expectations and needs. It would take twenty-two years of repeating the cycle of expectation and disappointment before I was willing to see Robert as he was, rather than as I wanted him to be.

MAINE—THE WAY LIFE WILL BE

SOUTHWEST HARBOR 1988

The drive from New York City to Mount Desert Island took the better part of a day. Robert drove. The first part of the drive out of the city was just something to be endured: congested highways, the BQE to 95 North to 91 up to Hartford. Then 84 going east to the Mass Pike briefly before heading north through the old mill towns of Worcester, Lowell, and Lawrence. By the time you reach the bridge that connects Portsmouth, New Hampshire, with Kittery, Maine, your journey is more than half over. But you still have a four-hour drive before you reach Mount Desert Island. Crossing the Piscataqua River is a significant mile marker, and the next one is the large sign that proclaims MAINE The Way Life Should Be. The first time I saw that sign it seemed prophetic. It was our first summer together, and there I was in Robert's car, the elegant, silver Mercedes convertible, with Robert at the wheel, driving toward Robert's childhood home—a place that meant so much to him that he organized his life so that he could spend whole summers there. I looked at the sign and saw *The Way Life Will Be*.

On a map Mount Desert Island looks like a big fat lobster claw, with Somes Sound practically splitting the two pieces apart. Its population of roughly ten thousand year-round residents swells to about four million over the summer months. Most of those are transient visitors to Acadia National Park, but quite a number are summer residents, some of whose families have been trekking to the island for decades or even centuries.

Robert said, "It's the most beautiful place on Earth." I was predisposed to like it. I wanted to fit into Robert's life, and I wasn't going to debate the point, but I thought, To you, of course, it is the most beautiful place. But there are so many spectacular, breathtaking places in the world, I'm not sure that Mount Desert is *the* most beautiful. If you had grown up on a verdant hillside on the west coast of Ireland, you would say it was the most beautiful. I didn't grow up in Ireland, but often wished I had.

My childhood summers had been spent in southern New England. We took day trips to Horseneck Beach, at the entrance to Cape Cod, and passed weeks at a time on Prudence Island in Narragansett Bay. For me the smell of summer was a pungent mixture of salt water, sand, and suntan lotion warmed by the sun. The sensations were of walking across the searingly hot pavement of the parking lot toward the sand dunes, encumbered by beach chairs, towels, picnic coolers, and straw bags filled with books, a camera, and sunglasses. On our arrival, the trek from the car to the water's edge would be full of energy and eager anticipation. After hours lying in the sun, bodysurfing the waves, and burying each other up to our necks in sand, my brothers and sisters and I would struggle back to the car, exhausted from the day, too tired to talk unless it was to crankily quarrel about not having enough room in the back seat.

When we were on Prudence Island we would traipse over the equally hot and sharp basalt rocks that created the cove where we swam. Diving off the cliff edge and swimming out to the raft, we would try to rock it enough to dump each other off, or engage in jellyfish fights, flinging the little blobs at each other that would dry like egg whites to a crackly finish on our skin.

Maine was none of these things. Maine was water too cold to swim in. It was fog, which would come and go without warning, or linger for weeks. Maine was the smell of pine tree sap and salty seaweed, and mud flats at low tide, which at first waft seemed like raw sewage but then seemed more honest, less rank. Maine was cormorants and loons swimming with the seagulls, white clapboard farmhouses with towers of lobster pots stacked in the yard, and on the outskirts of the farther islands, pods of seals basking on rocks in the sun. On still, overcast days, Maine was porpoises, slicing through the water, usually in pairs.

Maine was a life spent on the water. It was lobster boats and lobster traps and lobster buoys, lobster pounds and lobster dinners with a side of steamed clams at Thurston's in Bass Harbor. It was the fresh crabmeat sold at Sawyer's Market in Southwest Harbor that had been picked out and packaged at the local plant. Sawyer's Market was the first stop we made the first time Robert brought me to the island. It was the first stop on every return visit. It was owned and operated by Robert's friend Brian. There was a photo over the register of Brian's dad, jolly bald Don, in his butcher's apron with a broadly smiling Julia Child. It was the only celebrity photo on the wall, and when I first saw it in 1986, it was already a decade old. Turned out Julia Child summered on Mount Desert and had been a good friend of Robert's mother.

Sawyer's was a barometer of change as every summer we would return to see what had been replaced over the winter. But the old worn wood floors and the glass and white enameled metal meat counter (the first things you saw when you walked in from the street) never altered. Don retired to be replaced by mustachioed Dick, equally friendly but soon outdone by my own brother-in-law, Mark, a fourth-generation butcher from Searsport, and a Dom DeLuise look-alike. Sawyer's was a local market. It opened at 5:30 a.m. so that the contractors, boatyard workers, and landscapers could get their coffee, but it catered to the summer residents and the cruising crowd that chartered their boats from Hinckley's and had their groceries delivered to the dock. Over the years we learned to provision our basics in New York: olive oil, balsamic vinegar, espresso. For us, these were essentials, and expensive at Sawyer's, but we still stopped in daily. It was the only place to buy meat cut to order, and the big chunk of cheddar—*Rat Cheese,* the sign read—and Triscuits that were staples of Robert's summer diet.

This was Robert's Maine. For him, Mount Desert Island meant Southwest or Manset or maybe Bernard, the towns on the so-called quiet side. Southwest Harbor, on the southwest side of Somes Sound, is home to the island's largest year-round community, and it is also where he lived until he went away to school.

When I met Robert, he owned a two-bedroom cottage in Bernard, one of the small, mostly year-round fishing villages on the back side of the island. The town wasn't much more than a post office and a collection of simple peaked-roof farmhouses. The nearest grocery store was a convenience mart attached to a two-pump gas station in Tremont, three miles away. But the real estate was affordable. That, our friend Wendy pointed out, was because all the mosquitoes on Mount Desert congregated at the head of the cove.

Haywood lived next door. There was a well-trod path through the wild rose bushes, as Haywood would wander over every morning to sit on the porch with Robert and talk about cars and boats over coffee and doughnuts. He grew up in South Carolina, but he and Vicki sailed into Southwest Harbor in the summer of 1970, and toward the end of August when most summer visitors were packing their cars or sailboats and heading south, they stayed. The men were two of a pair as they sat in their deck chairs, dressed in well-worn Docksiders, khakis, and crew neck sweaters, their feet crossed at the ankles and propped on the porch railing.

The cottage stood at the head of Bass Harbor on a tidal cove, which dried out twice a day. There was a rickety dock, and occasionally Robert would tie up *Raven* and let her sit in the mud when the tide ran out. Mostly, he kept her at Chummy's Boatyard, farther out in the harbor, because his favorite way to pass the time was to explore the waters of his childhood.

With a cooler packed with Heinekens and tuna fish sandwiches, Robert could spend the better part of a day on the water. Motor out of the harbor, take a right, and head over to Swan's Island. If he took a left past Bass Harbor Light and along the Seawall shore with Great Cranberry Island to starboard, he'd enter Southwest Harbor and cruise up Somes Sound. "The only fjord in America," he'd say. Though the rocky shore and the dark water there were forbidding, Robert knew you could take a boat in as close to shore as the lobster pots were set. He could tell how the tide was running by the swirl of water around the bell buoys. He could tell which direction the wind was blowing by the swing of boats at anchor. To someone who didn't grow up on the coast of Maine knowing these things, it seemed like indecipherable secret code.

Raven was twenty-eight feet long, open to the weather, and all wood. She was powered by a huge 600 hp Chrysler engine that sat in the center of the boat and was covered by a teak box that doubled as seating. Robert had moved the steering column from the bow to the midship area, just in front of the engine box. *Raven,* though beautiful to look at it, was known as a wet boat. Depending on the direction of the wind, and the direction of travel, the spray from the chop would suddenly douse her passengers. She didn't glide through the water as much as muscle through it. If the weather was wet and foul, a canvas dodger, its plastic window long ago turned opaque and useless, could be pulled up to offer some protection over the seating in the bow of the boat. We would huddle together on the narrow bench seats under the dodger while Robert stood exposed to the weather, peering over the hood to navigate. There were many boat rides that started off sunny and dry and ended up wet and foggy. I always wore a sweater and a fleece, and often a windbreaker over that.

The waters of Mount Desert, the Western Way, and Penobscot Bay are as famous for the quickly changing weather as for the inhospitable rocky coastline and pine tree–covered islands. Dense, thick, white fog can roll in with little warning and at such speed that even with a navigation system boating can test the temperament of the most experienced sailors.

One of Robert's favorite destinations was Center Harbor. At one end was the town of Brooklin, home to *Wooden Boat* magazine and famous for the Center Harbor 31, an elegant sliver of a sailboat. At the other end, the mouth of the Benjamin River emptied into Penobscot Bay. In the middle was the Center Harbor Yacht Club, a one-story shingle bungalow, which was usually left unlocked and had a working toilet, a wonderful convenience I counted on, since all *Raven* offered was a cedar bucket. The harbor was buffered by Chatto Island, a pine-covered rocky outcropping about a quarter-mile long.

On a sunny, clear, warm, summer morning we left Bass Harbor and headed west toward Center Harbor. Our one-year-old daughter stayed behind with the babysitter. The trip usually took about an hour and a half. We had lunch, drinks, and a package of Milanos, Robert's favorite Pepperidge Farm cookie. Even well away from shore, it was warm enough for me to take off my sweater. It was going to be a perfect day out on the water.

As usual, Robert was at the helm, and I stood next to him to feel the wind blowing hard against my face. I held on to the dodger frame with one hand and wrapped my other arm around his waist. We didn't talk much; between the wind and the roar of the engine, words just got carried away. As we neared Naskeag Point outside of Center Harbor, Robert slowed the boat, and as he always did, he pointed out High Head.

"That's the summer home of the Bemis family. You know—the toilet seat? That's how they made their fortune." He loved to note who owned what and how they made their money. This one from textiles, that one from railroads. I was bemused by Robert's attention to the source of other people's wealth. Was it voyeuristic? A litmus test of a sort? In the early 1990s, "new" money was just beginning to show up. Within a few years, Martha Stewart would purchase a home in Seal Harbor.

The coast of Maine runs diagonally west to east. "Going Downeast" is moving north toward Canada. We were traveling west, which I, not being from around there, persisted in calling south. We passed Chatto Island on the starboard side and entered the harbor. It was full of boats. A sailboat that Robert used to own, and was still enamored of, was moored there. *Slipper* was the kind of boat that wooden-boat people got sentimental about. Every time we came to Center Harbor, Robert would look for her. We cruised around her slowly. Robert cut the motor and we ate our sandwiches as *Raven* drifted in the lee of the island. By three, we decided to head back. We would have just enough time before the babysitter had to leave.

As we left the harbor and came around Chatto we noticed the weather had changed. It was cooler now; I put my sweater on. The sea, which had been smooth on the ride down, was getting choppy. The clear day had turned blurry around the edges. That, I soon realized, was because we were headed into a wall of fog. Cool air over warm water or land causes the moisture in the air to condense. Fog can come or go within a matter of minutes, or it can hang around for days.

I'd weathered plenty of foggy days in the five years I'd been coming to Maine with Robert, but I'd never been caught out in it in a boat. At first Robert didn't think it was that thick, but as we plowed ahead, looking behind us, Chatto Island had vanished. The bright sunny day had turned gray and menacing. I wanted to turn back. I was trying to be brave, but common sense told me this was nuts. "We can't see anything. How can we navigate?" I pleaded with Robert. He agreed to turn back long enough to get his bearings.

"Take the charts out from under the seat," he said. "And check in the aft locker. I think the box with my dividers and rulers is stowed there. If I can get my bearings off Chatto, we'll be able to chart the course home. This isn't a big deal," he said soothingly.

Charting a course on a nautical map is not like reading a road map. First of all, math is involved. Having paper and pencil handy makes the job easier. The chart shows the land and all the marker and bell buoys. The bell buoys mark water hazards such as rocks or sandbars; the marker buoys denote the entrance to a harbor. Red right returning was the mnemonic Robert taught me; it meant keep the red buoy on your right when you're returning to the harbor. To get from Chatto to Bass Harbor required passage through Eggemoggin Reach, a thoroughfare leading to open ocean, dotted with islands. Spectacular in good weather. An ordeal in the fog.

Robert asked me if I could take the wheel and keep *Raven* at the compass points he gave me. With a job to do and Robert being so calm, I tried to shake off my unease. He spread the charts out on the engine box and began to figure things out. Dividers look like metal chopsticks that are connected at the top. Using them and the latitude scale on the chart it's possible to measure the distance in nautical miles. One minute equals one mile. The plastic parallel ruler is used to plot direction. It's complicated, and it might have been a few years since Robert last had to navigate blind, but he obviously knew what he was doing.

It was still daytime, though it felt like twilight. The hour-and-a-half trip stretched to two and a half. We motored slowly, feeling our way, trying to spot the lobster buoys before we ran over them. In the fog, sound is amplified. We listened for air horns from other boats, a sharp bleating sound that punctures the silence. We listened for the deep chugging thrum of lobster boats and for the echoing clang of the bell buoys. Fog also seems to amplify smells, and the salt air seemed tangier, sharper, fishier. And fog is wet: after an hour my sweater and hair were damp.

The closer we could get to shore, the more likely we were to see something and get our bearings. But getting close to shore risked running into rocks. As we neared Bass Harbor, the shoreline suddenly loomed into view off our port side. The fog was lifting—I was weepy with relief. My hands were cold and stiff from gripping the wheel too tightly.

Robert came and stood beside me, draping his arm over my shoulders. Giving me a hug and a smile, he asked if I wanted him to take over. "Gladly," I said. I was starstruck by his ability. I'd been so sure we were doomed, but Robert knew what he was doing. Navigating through the fog wasn't a big deal to him.

DRINKING

NEW YORK CITY 1989; MAINE 1991

I used to dwell on Robert's death. On the likelihood. The inevitability. He seemed to be asking for it. At first my imaginings were driven by fear, anxiety, dread. Later, those mixed with spiteful fantasy.

If I woke up at 3 a.m. and he was not in bed next to me, I was sure he'd been mugged, or worse, as he barhopped his way around Lower Manhattan. My thoughts were as vivid as a gritty TV crime series: the attack as he walked in a dark alleyway, the screech of tires and sickening thud as a speeding car he didn't see careened into him, the altercation at the pool hall when he beat his opponent. *Law & Order* had nothing on my imagination.

When we lived in New York City, I could plot his evening's passage by the hour he came in. Two a.m.: he'd come straight home from the Odeon, the restaurant in Tribeca where so much of our romance had played out, and where a small group of us ended the night after our wedding reception on the Upper East Side. Three a.m.: he had moved on to the Ear Inn, the somewhat seedy bar on Spring Street near the West Side Highway, with a back room full of pool tables. Five a.m.: his last stop, one of the after-hours bars in the meatpacking district, where transvestites and drag queens were still trolling the sidewalks at the first hint of daylight.

For a few years, after McCullough was born, we lived year-round in Maine, and if he were late coming home from work, I would be convinced he'd had a car accident. He never did, but I knew what it would be like.

A squeal of tires, a brutal thud as the vehicle plowed into the trunk of a spruce tree, the shattering of glass, the blare of a horn stuck in alarm mode. It happened one night, just down the road from our house. The not-so-young driver staggered out of the car, blood dripping from a gash on his forehead. He'd been drinking.

Standing in the kitchen, with our baby daughter in her high chair, feeding her dinner, I would stare out the window into the eerie darkness of an early winter's night. The only visible sign of life, the blinking red light of the bell buoy far offshore. The dark, the cold and damp seemed to forecast only bad things. It was 6 p.m. Robert worked for an architect in Bar Harbor. Where was he? He should be home by now. I would call his office.

"Helen? It's Tara. Is Robert still there?"

"No."

"Do you know what time he left?"

"Oh, at least an hour ago."

I felt humiliated making the call. I didn't like what it implied about Robert—or me. It was a half-hour drive from the office in Bar Harbor to the farmhouse we were renting in Southwest. There weren't many places he could stop along the way. But there was the Porcupine Grill, and there was his drinking buddy, Duane.

When he breezed in after I'd put our daughter to bed, it was without explanation or excuse. He would look at me as my concern gave way to anger and ask, "What's wrong with you?"

"You should've called. I didn't know where you were. I called the office and Helen said you left hours ago."

"You're not my mother," he would say dismissively.

"You're right. I'm not your mother. I'm your wife. I'm someone who loves and cares about you. I'm not giving you a curfew, Robert! I'm just asking you to be considerate. I just want to know that you're okay."

"Why wouldn't I be?" he would say as he walked out of the room.

I heard stories of drunks dying horrible, premature deaths as evidence of what would happen to Robert when his luck ran out. There was the sailor, living on his boat in Hadlock Cove near Islesford, who was found one morning under it. He'd been drinking with friends on another sailboat moored in the harbor, and they guessed that after he rowed himself back to his boat, he must have slipped as he climbed aboard. The rope from the dinghy caught around his ankle so he was tethered in his watery grave.

There was a man in Northeast Harbor who owned one of the old, shingled cottages that perched on the cliff overlooking Bear Island. One night during a thunderstorm the house caught fire. It was a lightning strike, and it took out the phone service. The man was home alone, drinking. He was said to have been frantic. But he got into his car, a Hummer, and tore up the twisty roads to get help. He crashed on the corner by the Asticou, plowing into Cranberry Cottage. He was arrested for drunk driving at the same time that his house was burning to the ground. A few years later, we heard he died in a bar in Mexico, impaled on a toilet plunger. He'd slipped in the bathroom while puking into the toilet bowl, and the plunger went through his eye, into his brain.

Alcohol had the upper hand in our relationship from the start, though I didn't know it. When Robert and I first met, we were swept along in a tide of alcohol. One didn't have to exert much energy or make any effort to swim in that ocean. We were buoyed by cocktails, wine, Cognac, and Heinekens purchased at the corner deli at 3 a.m., on our way home from the Odeon. Everybody knows that booze makes everything look brighter, easier, funnier. Until, of course, it doesn't anymore. It's hard to believe that neither of us had a clue about alcohol abuse, and its effect on us. Our attraction to each other was electric, the sex sizzling and unfettered. Our disagreements, loud and unruly. It was all so hot and fired up, yet it never occurred to either of us that the fuel to that fire was alcohol.

And it never occurred to me not to drink. It was habitual. It was historical. At my grandfather's house in Providence, the bar was a cluster of crystal decanters in the pantry. Each bottle wore a little metal necklace around its neck, declaring its name: *Rye, Whiskey, Scotch, Bourbon.* There were specific glasses for different drinks: highballs, lowballs, *v*-shaped fishbowls for martinis, different-sized glasses for sherry, red wine, white wine, and champagne.

My grandfather would arrive home from work—he was an insurance lawyer—precisely at 5:30, and he and my mother would convene in the living room with a plate of Triscuits and cheddar cheese for cocktails: for him, a Scotch on the rocks; for my mother, a glass of white wine. He had rescued his daughter-in-law and six grandchildren (my mother, my brothers and sisters, and me) from an abusive marriage.

In the summers my mother and her sisters and all the cousins would gather on Prudence Island, in an old Victorian cottage that Grandfather had purchased on a whim. It was a household of women, overseen by my mother's mother, Grandmere. Fun and games, competitions to see who could do the dinner dishes in record time, massive games of hide-and-seek after dark; everything had a lighthearted air. My Aunt Grace kept an eye on the time. At 5 p.m. sharp, she would announce cocktails. Gin and tonics for the grown-ups. Bitter lemon for the kids. This was what normal was.

Decades later I would remember those days not for what happened but by the undercurrents that flowed around us; my mother and her sisters were all divorced or separated, deserted by disappointing men.

We children were mostly raising ourselves, a motley gang of teenagers looking after our younger siblings. In hindsight, the drinking seems less like a party and more like an escape. No wonder I was drawn to Robert.

Despite my fears of an accident, Robert was, in fact, a very good driver, even when drunk. Even before learning to drive a race car. Living in Maine, or actually anywhere outside of New York City, meant driving to restaurants, and then a couple of hours and more than a few drinks later, driving home. It was routine. He was expert.

A favorite destination in the summer was a French country bistro, off-island. It was a 1940s-style inn on the side of a two-lane highway between Ellsworth and Winter Harbor. If you drove by it in the middle of the day, if you even noticed it, you would think, "Who would eat there?" At night, with the small parking areas on either side of the building overflowing with cars, and warm light radiating out, it existed as its own little world, removed from the nowhereville of poor backwoods Maine.

Robert and I went to Le Domaine a few times every summer, even though it was never a simple or inexpensive affair. It was an outing, an adventure. He'd taken me there on my first visit to the island. We'd sat at a large table for two in a corner of the dining room. Robert ordered rosé Champagne, which I'd never had, and a dozen oysters on the half-shell for us to share. They were small and briny and harvested nearby. He preferred mignonette to the thick ketchup and horseradish sauce, which, he explained, smothered the taste. He showed me how to slide the fork under the body of the oyster to make sure it was free of the muscle holding it to its shell. And then putting the little fork aside, he raised the shell to his lips and sucked the body into his mouth, careful not to lose any of the brine. He uttered an audible "Aah." Robert's enjoyment of food was vocal.

One night, unusually warm for July, a year or so after we were married, we put the top down on the convertible for the drive over to Le Domaine. I had a pashmina to keep me warm, and Robert, despite his devotion to his grubby everyday khakis and frayed polo shirts, dressed for dinner. In the car I imagined myself Grace Kelly in *To Catch A Thief.* Robert was my Cary Grant. He wore a lightweight gray silk blazer he'd bought on our first trip together to Italy, a button-down shirt, lightweight wool trousers, and loafers without socks. Robert could look effortlessly elegant when he gave it a bit of thought.

It was the usual over-the-top Le Domaine evening. Lovely food with a different drink for every course: Champagne with the oysters, a bottle of Burgundy with the roast duck, and Cognac after the crème brulee.

When we left the restaurant, we kept the top down on the convertible. The bite of salt air and the chill of the night were a perfect antidote to the floating feeling of having had too much to drink. As we came across the causeway onto the island, we saw rows of flashing lights and a line of traffic ahead of us. The state troopers had set up a sobriety checkpoint. Robert tensed. I had had just as much to drink. It was better for him to be behind the wheel. We considered turning around, but the only way onto the island, the only way home, was via the causeway and through the checkpoint.

Robert said, "Let me handle this. Don't say anything unless they talk to you."

He slowed the car and, as we neared the roadblock, one of them signaled for him to stop. The trooper approached.

"May I see your license and registration, please?"

I opened the glove box and fished them out.

"Where are you coming from?" he asked, as Robert handed him the papers.

"Le Domaine in Hancock."

The trooper studied the documents and handed them back. "Have you had anything to drink?"

"Just two glasses of wine with dinner," Robert lied.

The trooper considered him. Then he looked at me. I smiled trying to look relaxed. Robert was composed, calm.

"Have a safe drive home." The trooper waved us on.

Neither of us said a word until we could no longer see the blue lights behind us, and then Robert exhaled in relief. "God, that was close." I think Robert and I feared the write-up in the *Bar Harbor Times*'s police blotter the most. It was the most popular part of the weekly paper, as residents of the island turned to that page first to see which of their neighbors had gotten into trouble, and for what. We knew it was a narrow escape. By the next morning, when I heard Robert telling the story to Haywood over coffee, the relief had turned to laughter. It was another story to add to the archives, just more evidence that the tide of luck ran with Robert.

"Remember the night Robert got lost in the fog with Duane?" His friends would retell the story endlessly. They were glad not to have been on the boat with him. They would never have done something so foolish. But they talked merrily about his exploits.

"I can't imagine a worse person to be lost in the fog with than Duane," his friend John laughed. Duane was a forty-five-year-old overgrown jock from someplace like Mississippi or Alabama. How he ended up living on the coast of Maine was a mystery to us.

Robert and I were going to dinner in Seal Harbor with Duane and his girlfriend of the moment. It was a warm, clear night so Robert proposed motoring over in *Raven*.

"It's a perfect night for a sunset cruise," Robert said. "I'll take Duane and his girlfriend, and you can drive the car over to Chez Wendy, so we can all drive home."

"What about the boat?" I asked.

"It's fine to leave it tied up at the town dock overnight. We can get it in the morning."

The boat trip over to Seal Harbor took about thirty minutes. I can see Robert standing at the helm—radiating elegance and confidence. He wore unpressed khakis and beat-up boat shoes, dressed up with a blue blazer; his tortoise-shell glasses glinted in the early evening light, and his silver hair, already receding from his brow but still luxurious and wavy, was long enough to brush his collar. He would have been keeping an eye out for lobster buoys and other boats, but he would have been half-turned toward his companions, naming the islands and other points of interest they passed on the way to Seal Harbor.

After dinner and several bottles of wine, Robert and Duane thought it would be fun to take the boat back.

"There's just enough moonlight," Robert said. Girlfriend rolled her eyes.

"It's too cold for me," she said. "I'll drive home with Tara."

Duane said, "Bet we beat you home!"

The route from Seal Harbor back to our house afforded many views of the water. Passing by the head of the harbor in Southwest, I could see that it was now shrouded in fog. Houses and boats had disappeared; only ghostly halos of light penetrated the gloom, suggesting life. But whether these lights were on land or water, I couldn't tell.

"That's not good," Girlfriend said.

"Robert knows his way around," I assured her. "I bet if they see a dock, they'll just tie up. He'll call the house and tell us where they are."

Back at home, there was no message on the answering machine. Like many of Robert's escapades, this happened in the era before cell phones. There was nothing for us to do but fret and wait.

It was after 2 a.m., when at last we heard the crunch of gravel in the driveway.

Robert's first words to me as he walked in the door were, "You didn't call the Coast Guard, did you?"

"Of course, I did!"

He berated me. "Don't ever do that. That was stupid. I was perfectly okay."

He was concerned that if they'd found him, they would have realized he'd been drinking. In fact, the Coast Guard didn't raise the alarm. It seemed their policy was not to rush right out to rescue drunken sailors.

WOODING *RAVEN*

SOUTHWEST HARBOR, MAINE
FALL/WINTER/SPRING 1991–92

"You need a job," Robert says. We've decided to give living in Maine year-round a try. "What are you going to do?" he asks.

"What do you mean? I thought we agreed I was going to take care of McCullough." She's just turned one.

Robert doesn't respond. We're sitting on the porch looking out to the harbor, which is still full of boats. *Raven* is tied up at Chummy's. In just a few more weeks she'll be hauled out for the winter.

"You could wood *Raven*. I've been talking with Chummy about getting on his schedule. She needs to be wooded, and I think you could do it."

"What are you talking about?"

"I mean it. It might take a while, but I think you could do it. And think of the money we'd save. It will cost ten thousand if we have Chummy do it."

"Robert, I barely know what wooding is, much less how to do it."

"Basically, it's just taking off the old varnish and then giving her ten new coats. You steel-wool the varnish between each coat."

"Oh, is that all?" I laugh. I look at Robert. He meets my gaze. "Oh my god, you're serious."

"Well, you have to do something," he says again.

"Taking care of McCullough is something."

We'd returned to Maine at the beginning of the summer from Los Angeles, where I'd had a good job at an entertainment company. We'd left because Robert couldn't find work and spent his days playing tennis and drinking martinis at lunch, while a babysitter looked after McCullough. I'd taken a short maternity leave after she was born. Now, I'm looking forward to taking care of her myself.

I resent the double standard. Apparently, it's okay for Robert to not work, and not take care of our child, but not only should I take care of our child—I should also do something else as well.

Why does Robert feel I need to do something more than look after McCullough? Living in Maine is a lot less expensive than living in LA. Is it about the money? Or is it about who controls the purse strings? Robert has a trust fund. I don't. I guess I have to earn my keep. I don't say any of that. I don't have the heart for a full-blown argument just now. I switch tactics and focus on the logistics.

"First, where would I do it? Second, I can just hear the comments from people around here: '*She* thinks she can wood a boat?' You're always so concerned about what the locals think. And what about McCullough? Who's going to take care of her if I'm at the boatyard?"

"I bet we can rent space from Chummy, and you can do it inside over the winter. Chummy will help you out if you get stuck. And you can get childcare a few days a week." Robert seems determined to have me wood *Raven*.

A wooden boat with a lot of brightwork needs to have the varnish refreshed every year. It was one of Robert's jobs when he was a dock boy in the summer at his father's boatyard. But wooding a boat—stripping it down to bare wood and then applying layer after layer of varnish—is a magnitude of difference from what he'd done as a kid.

When I was twelve years old, I'd refinished an oak desk my mother gave me for my birthday. It was a delicate piece, with curvy legs, a drop front, one large drawer, and a set of cubbyholes, but it was painted brown, and I wanted to see the oak grain. I'd assembled my tools: Zip-Strip, an empty metal can, paint brushes, steel wool, fine-grade sandpaper, a screwdriver, an old toothbrush, clear varnish. It had taken me months working on it after school out in the barn, and when the weather turned cold, my mother and I moved it down to the basement so I could finish it over the winter. That childhood memory gave me just a hint of what I might be letting myself in for.

"Okay, if you think I can, I'll give it a shot." I feel myself rising to the challenge. The pleasure of being on *Raven* and seeing the world from across her glossy teak decks sometimes made the destination irrelevant. Robert was immensely proud of owning *Raven*. I wanted her to be *our* boat. I thought, by wooding her I would earn the right.

We go see Chummy. A lifelong resident of Bass Harbor, from a family of lifelong residents, he's a true islander, but without the usual town-and-gown resentments. He's good-humored with a round face that accommodates a perpetual smile, that gets broader when he hears Robert's plan. He has an available boat shed. "You can use the upper bay. *Raven* will just fit in. There's a Modine heater, but it can be drafty." He's sizing me up. I imagine him thinking: city girls with nail polish don't work in boatyards. But he's willing to go along with us.

By the time I start work on *Raven* it's November and already feeling like winter. The crystalline fall days have passed. Gray skies and pervasive damp are the near-daily forecast. The boatyard is mostly deserted. If someone's around, I often search through several buildings to find them.

Raven sits in a cradle, a construction of metal bars that hold her high off the ground. Even out of the water she's a beautiful boat. Twenty-eight feet long, and I don't know how many feet below the water line, her deck is probably fifteen feet in the air. I climb a ladder to get into the cockpit. This is my main workspace. She can easily hold twelve people when we take our picnic cruises in the summer. Two bench seats in the bow of the boat hold six, Robert at the wheel, of course, one or two sitting on the engine box, and a bench at the stern can seat three. Now I survey her differently. Every inch of wood will need to be restored. But first, I need to remove all the cleats, every strip of metal, the chrome edging, the hinges, the steering column, the exhaust vents—basically disassemble all the elements that make her a functioning boat.

I tear open a brown paper bag and draw a diagram, numbering and naming each item so I will know where it belongs when it's time to put it back. I add blue painter's tape and a Sharpie marker to my supplies list. I know how to do this: break everything down into manageable elements, systematically go through them, one step at a time.

Robert had already told me about needing fine steel wool, but that's for later. To get the old layers of paint and varnish off, I need something heavy-duty. I buy an electric sander that I can hold in one hand. The surface area is four by four inches, small enough to maneuver into corners and large enough to move along and make good progress when I work on the deck.

My first hurdle: years of saltwater and sea air have corroded the screws. Some of them pop out with a whisper of a touch; they will need to be replaced. Others refuse to budge, like bad clams that don't open even after they've been steamed. I abandon the hand-held screwdriver, reach for my power drill. All I manage to do is further strip the threads away. If Robert and I were doing this together, I could leave those for him. He had come with me to the boat shed early on to assess the project, but other than that time he rarely visits. The reality is sinking in. I've barely started, and already I'm feeling alone and defeated by three-quarter-inch bits of calcified metal.

"Never stop on a hill," my sister Ursula, the nurse, and a marathon runner said, as I slowed at the base of a long incline up. I was accompanying her on a training run. It was a sticky, hot summer's day. But we both laughed when she said it. It was code for Kellys Don't Quit. The harder, more uncomfortable it is—*it* can be anything—the more valuable the effort is. "Never stop on a hill" became my mantra for the next six months.

The repetitive and methodical nature of the work can be soothing or exhausting depending on my frame of mind. I spend a lot of time having conversations with myself. Me and whoever is occupying my thoughts, usually Robert. The specter of alcohol abuse has already appeared. He's taken to stopping off after work to have a drink with Duane before he comes home. Or more than one. I'm not loving life in Maine in the winter. At least in the city, when it gets dark early, you have the comfort of millions of lights. Now I wait at home, alone with McCullough, not sure where Robert is or when he'll come in. I pick up the thread from the argument of the night before, finding the words I wished I'd said instead of the ones I did. Rehearsing what I will say the next time. I know there will be a next time.

Robert and I have been married for three years and I'm still deeply enamored with him, but already disruptive cycles and patterns have emerged. Drinking, certainly. And money. This is a shock to me. How can someone who just inherited a lot of money from their mother, just a few years ago, have money problems. "It's not the lack of money," Robert said. "It's cash flow."

Here I am, all alone, in a dirty, cold boatyard on a godforsaken island off the coast of Maine in the dead of winter running a belt sander spewing fine particulate matter into my face, all to save Robert ten thousand dollars so he can buy another car. After he figures out his cash flow problem.

There are days I plan to work on the boat, but the weather dissuades me. Unexpectedly warm, and I want to take advantage of the respite and spend the day outdoors, not sequestered in a dreary dim boat shed. Gun-metal skies sputtering icy snowflakes, and I think I don't want to drive in a snowstorm; I'll go tomorrow instead.

Once I pull into the parking lot beside the boat shed, I won't leave until my shift is over. The novelty of wooding *Raven* has morphed from being an interesting challenge to lonely drudgery. It is dirty, hard work. I will also have to paint her sides and underneath. Below the water line gets a special kind of antifouling paint that's supposed to repel marine growth. It's highly toxic. Even as the days become shorter, the list of things that need to be done grows longer. I'm not just sanding down the teak decking and applying new varnish. This is a top-to-bottom restoration.

"How's it going over there?" Robert asks on a near-daily basis when he gets home from the office.

"Did you work on *Raven* today? You know I want her in the water before Memorial Day. Will she be ready?"

"You know, Tara, I think you're going to have to put in more than a couple of hours on the days McCullough's in daycare, if you're going to finish on time."

That one gets me. It's classic. This from the guy who didn't do anything but play tennis the nine months we lived in LA. Even though I'm wooding *Raven*, I'm still taking care of all the housework, shopping, cooking. If it needs to be done, I'm doing it.

I sense that Robert does not view my wooding *Raven* as a labor of love, for him or for the boat, just as a contribution toward our finances. I'm feeling less like a partner and more like a hired hand doing hard manual labor. Only I'm not getting paid.

"I'd like to see you wood *Raven*!"

"I never said I could, would, or wanted to."

"I don't remember ever saying I *wanted* to either."

Robert answers the way he so often does; he refills his wineglass and walks out of the room. I'll replay this exchange for days, my aggravation turning into aggression as I attack the work on the boat.

Why isn't Robert helping me on the weekends if he's so concerned that I won't finish by *his* deadline? He doesn't offer. And I resent him for it, but I'll be damned if I'll ask him to. Is it because I want to be able to say I did it all by myself? Or I don't want to open myself up to more criticism? I'm probably not doing it the way he would. Better to keep him away since he only seems interested in the result, not the process.

Winter turns into spring, though the boat shed holds the chill, and I often wear a hat and open-fingered gloves while I work. In an effort to warm up, I eat my lunch outside in the sun. I see the end in sight the day I start to varnish. I want to celebrate, but I'm afraid my enthusiasm will be met with skepticism. Still, the hardest part is over. Speculation about whether I could do it has switched to whether I'll be done in time for *Raven*'s launch on Memorial Day.

A good varnish job looks clear as glass. The steady hand applying it and a clean work environment are both essential to a good result. The decades of dirt that has settled in the boat shed is easily stirred up. On a windy day the single-paned windows rattle in their casings and drafts blow in through the cracks in the walls. I don't varnish on those days. But slowly, the bits and pieces of the boat, the coaming, the decks, the gunwales begin to take on a luster. *Raven* is coming back to life. Better than that, *I* am bringing her back to life.

Then I have a serious setback. The coaming, a vertical surface that runs around the circumference of the cockpit, is made of a wide-grain oak. Somehow, I thought it might match the teak better if I stained it a red oak color. Even as I apply it, watching the stain seep deep into the wood as though it were a dry sponge, I have a twinge of misgiving, but tell myself, it's probably just because it's wet. It will look better when it's dry. I finish the entire length before I leave for the night.

The next morning as I climb the ladder into *Raven,* I see that I should have listened to that inner voice. I should have stopped when I thought it looked wrong. The coaming is as bright red as my grandmother's lipstick. I can't hold back the tears, but what the hell, why should I? There's no one else here. No one to see me or to console me. I'm tired of doing this by myself, undone by both the setback and what is still on the list to complete. Mad at myself for not saying no in the first place and mad at Robert for making it my job. It's all too much. I know the coaming will have to be redone. But not now. I walk away.

When I confess to Robert that I've messed up, he says, "Maybe it's not so bad." He thinks I'm overreacting. "Come and look at it then," I say.

"We can live with it," he says when we go to the boatyard that weekend. But I know we can't. Or at least I can't. Maybe his giving me permission to live with it makes me more determined to fix it.

After I redo the coaming, which I calculate set me back at least a week, I start to lose interest. I wouldn't mind turning the job over to Chummy's crew. I've had enough. My pride is willing to take a back seat to my exhaustion. But I don't say that, and the moment passes. The weather's improving, which makes working on the boat less disagreeable but also makes me want to be elsewhere—hiking or doing anything at all outside with McCullough. I've given *Raven* eight coats of blemish-free varnish. I decide that will have to be enough. I polish and refasten all the chrome. I paint her sides a bright white, the floor a classic gray, and her hull a sea green.

We launch her at the end of May. Haywood brings a bottle of champagne to crack over her bow like they do when they christen big ships. Turns out it would likely scratch or damage the varnish, or dent the wood, and I have too much invested to risk that. We just toast with it instead.

All that summer, Robert will tell friends and visitors, when they board *Raven* that I'd done the brightwork. "Tara spent the winter wooding *Raven*," he says. If they don't know what that means, he'll explain in detail, giving me credit for the long hours and hard labor. I'll smile and agree that it had been a lot of work.

"I don't think I would have let him talk me into it if I'd known what a big job it was going to be," I'll say. I will repeat that line many times in the years to come. Saying yes when I could have said no. Helping Robert fulfill his dreams, or acquiescing to his latest desire, became something I took pride in, even as I resented him for continually raising his expectations of what I would accept. Even when I recognized I was being coerced or when I felt put upon, I still agreed.

In the years to come Robert would ask me to help him open a restaurant (twice), ask me to give up a job I loved to help him run the restaurant, ask me to say yes to this scheme and that purchase, ask me to trust him with drinking and trust him with our finances. And each time I would say yes, but with conditions. It was never a happy yes. I existed as a moderator of impulses and enforcer of our agreements. The voice of reason in the face of his unrealistic expectations, but still very much by his side. It never occurred to me that maybe he wouldn't go ahead if he didn't have me along for the ride. I felt like I was both protecting him and protecting our family, from his worst impulses, while encouraging his best. I think

there's a phrase for that: playing God, magical thinking, enabling.
I had as much of an overinflated sense of my abilities as I thought
Robert did of his. We were executing an unconscious dance without
knowing the steps. A waltz of wills with selective blindness. I can't
blame Robert that it took me so long to break away and say, "No. I
think I'll sit this one out."

SAILING

Practically the first question Robert asked me when we met was, "Do you like to sail?" I instinctively recognized it as a kind of test. On one level the question was, "Do you know how to sail?" To answer yes would indicate that my life afforded me access to boats and summers spent on the water. To take the question at face value, he was asking, "Do you and I have something in common?" This man was very appealing. He oozed confidence and security about his place in the world. I wanted to share something in common with him. Instead of a direct answer, I told him a story.

My parents were teenagers when they met as camp counselors at adjoining sailing camps in Rhode Island. My mother stayed passionate about sailing, and as we grew up, she shipped her children off to these same camps. When I was eleven, it was my turn to go. Back then, awards and ribbons were given out for actual accomplishment. There were no soothing condolence prizes like "Tries the Hardest," "Only Capsized Three Times." Nothing like that.

I was most often teamed with the gutsiest sailor in our group, the girl who won the blue ribbons. She was probably my age, but I remember her as older, stronger, certainly braver. I lived in terror of falling out of the boat as she sailed close-hauled into the wind, the gunwales on one side practically in the water, and me, white-knuckled and nauseous, braced against the slant as we powered forward. At the end of an eternity—or was it only two weeks?—when the certificates were handed out at the last night's bonfire, I was the only camper who didn't get one. I'm sure I was embarrassed, maybe humiliated, but I was also vindicated. I didn't have to be a sailor.

Robert accepted the story as a challenge. He was sure that under his tutelage I would come to love it as he did.

Shortly after Robert and I met, before I ever went to Maine with him, we took a trip to St. Michael's on the Eastern Shore of Maryland. We rented a little skiff, and as we tooled around the harbor, he pointed at a sailboat. "That's a Hinckley," he said. I found it hard to believe that he could recognize the designer of one boat over another. I was impressed but doubtful. It wasn't until much later that I realized anyone could tell a Hinckley because of the signature cove stripe that runs along the side, just below the gunwale. Years later, after many summers in Maine, I adopted the same air of knowingness when I would spot a Concordia, recognizable by its cove stripe with a star at the bow and a sliver of a moon at the stern.

The summer after we married, Robert chartered a 35-foot sailboat so he could teach me how to sail. We would cruise from Camden to Winter Harbor and back to Southwest. We invited my mother and my Uncle Brian to join us for a few days. With avid sailors onboard, I was able to dodge the high-pressure duties of first mate. I took refuge in the galley as the self-assigned cook, or if the day was warm, I would sunbathe up in the bow with a book. Robert didn't seem to notice or mind that I avoided taking the helm. His desire to teach me to sail gave way to his pleasure in being back on a sailboat that in truth was easy enough for him to handle on his own.

Five years later, the summer I was pregnant with Jack, Robert came home from having coffee with Haywood and announced he'd been given the chance to take a friend's Hinckley 42 out for a sail that afternoon. I was happy for him. It was a luxury cruising boat, but not what I would call a day sailer. At 42 feet it was double the length of the average living room. The mast was almost as tall (62 feet) as a five-story building. The sail area was more than 800 square feet. It seemed like a big responsibility.

"Will Haywood go with you?" I asked.

"No," Robert said. "He's busy. I thought you would come."

At two months pregnant, though not terribly sick, the last thing I wanted to do was go sailing. The very last thing I wanted to do was go sailing as Robert's first mate, on a borrowed yacht that he'd never sailed before. But I had a hard time saying, "No. Sorry. Can't. Don't want to." By two in the afternoon, I was usually ready for a nap. Instead,

at two o'clock I was walking down the gangway at Chummy's, filled
with dread, preparing to board the Sou'wester.

Much of that afternoon has receded to a dim memory. We managed
to cast off and motor out of Bass Harbor without incident or harsh
words. Once under way we headed toward Gott's Island. The wind
was stiff. It was a lot of boat to handle, and Robert reefed the sail. I
could see he was overwhelmed. He was never at his best in that state,
and now out of his depth he yelled at me.

"Grab that sheet! Pull it tight!"

"Sheet? Do you mean this rope? How tight?"

Robert's tension scared me. If he wasn't comfortable, if he couldn't
handle the boat, how could I help?

As Robert panicked and yelled at me, I yelled back and dissolved
in tears.

"This wasn't my idea. I didn't want to come in the first place!"

I held tight to the line as directed, not bothering to hide my tears.
Robert silently turned the boat toward home. This was not the time
for a sailing lesson. This was supposed to be fun. If I suffered from
not knowing when to say no, Robert did too. Offered the "chance
of a lifetime," he couldn't let it pass, even if the conditions were not
good for accepting it.

Quite often our reactions to our experiences were rooted in the situation.
We hadn't developed the ability to see the big picture, or to take the
long view. We both shared the attitude that the present could always be

improved upon. This led to high expectations and much disappointment when the imagined bliss failed to materialize.

So began a big life adjustment for both of us. I was the first woman in Robert's life who didn't like to sail and didn't naturally love the water. He had photo albums filled with pictures of Colby and him, looking happy and relaxed on their cruising boat *Tandria*. They'd sailed to Bermuda together. He had dreams of doing a transatlantic crossing. Clearly it wasn't going to be with me. I liked the ground under my feet. Swimming with my brothers and sisters in the summer was fun, but cold, dark water is scary. It wasn't just the power of a vast ocean that intimidated me; I don't care for ponds or lakes either.

No. I wasn't going to join him on a long-distance cruise, and no, I didn't enjoy sailing alone with him, but I loved Maine, and I loved cruising around in *Raven*. Why couldn't that be enough for Robert?

REHAB, RELAPSE, REPEAT

Robert diagnosed himself. It was early in our marriage, and we were living in Maine year-round. He was already in the bargaining stage of drinking. He'd say:

"No more cocktails before dinner."

"I'm only going to drink wine from now on, no hard liquor."

"Only two glasses of wine a night."

It was winter, and he sat alone at the bar of the Porcupine Grill, chasing down dinner with shots of Wild Turkey. I was away visiting friends. When he got home, he took out the *Mayo Clinic Health Guide,* a Christmas present from his sister. Fourteen hundred pages of maladies, disease, and afflictions. He looked up the definition of alcoholic. There are more than eighty references to alcohol and alcoholism in the index. He turned to page 422 and read the section on Recognizing the Alcoholic: "Experience reveals that alcoholism knows no social or economic bounds. Seemingly happy and successful people are just as likely to suffer from this disease as are those whose lives are filled with disappointments and failure. Many alcoholics are highly regarded people in society and pass for years among their friends and associates as healthy and normally functioning people."

Robert took the abbreviated version of the SAAST (Self-Administered Alcoholism Screening Test) on page 423, ten questions that reveal alcohol dependence. As he told me the story the next day on the phone, he sounded pleased that he'd scored high marks on the test. He was a gifted student and always expected to do well. His elation was short-lived. The Mayo book references a preoccupation with alcohol: "People who are alcohol dependent tend to look forward to the next time they will be able to drink. They may select social activities on the basis of whether alcohol is available." We were familiar with variations on that theme. We had friends who brought their own cocktail when they went to a party for fear that the host might not have their preferred drink. Robert nearly always brought a bottle of wine from his wine cellar figuring it would be better than what would be served, which meant he didn't really bring it as a house gift. It was more like, "Here, why don't you open this?"

My realization that he had a problem occurred a month before. Liquor stores in Maine were closed on Sundays. Back then, supermarkets didn't sell wine or beer. As I made dinner, Robert went to the wine cabinet and discovered we didn't have a single bottle in the house.

There was nothing to drink. It was clearly my fault. I did the shopping. "How could you let this happen?" His voice had an edge of hysteria.

I toggled back and forth from trying to help ––"Call Haywood, I'm sure he'll have something you can take"–– to resentment and challenge––"Are you actually going to fall apart because you can't have wine with dinner?" Our conversation was still shrouded in the veneer of sophistication that said wine with dinner didn't really count. Of course, if Robert was willing to admit that he was desperate for a drink, he would have walked down the street to a bar, but he wasn't quite there yet.

When Robert told me about the night at the Porcupine Grill (Wild Turkey + *Mayo Health Guide* = Alcoholism), I was so proud of him. Clever, smart Robert. Problem solved. Except identifying a problem and being ready to deal with it were two different things. He quickly began to backpedal. Nothing terrible had happened. No car crash. No DUI. He was lonely, vulnerable, and experiencing an introspective soul-searching moment, which he soon regretted sharing with me. Less than a day later denial set in.

"It was the Wild Turkey. If I'd only been drinking wine, it would have been okay."

"It's because I was alone. If you'd been with me, I wouldn't have drunk so much."

The trouble with awareness is that you can't pretend you didn't have it. Sharing his diagnosis with me Robert invited me to be, at best, a support as he sought ways to curb his drinking and, at worst, a witness to his inability to control it. As his wife, with a stake in the stability and happiness of our family, I was sympathetic, but my inherent nature is to be a problem solver. My view was, once you've identified a problem, you're under a moral obligation to solve it, or at least try. It would take me a long time to understand that Robert's alcoholism was not a problem I could solve. As his interest in admitting to, dealing with, or solving the problem ebbed and flowed, the conditions for periodic squalls and storms hung around our periphery like the fog off the shore of Greenings. Not to torture the weather metaphor but much of our life together was spent in a sea-smoke haze of misapprehension and misunderstanding.

Robert said, "I'm an alcoholic." Then later, "How do you or I know if I'm an alcoholic?" "What's the definition?" or "I know I drink too much, but that doesn't mean I'm an alcoholic." As we learned more about alcoholism, through therapists, doctors, and friends, the definition only became cloudier. Drinking buddies were defensive. "Don't be ridiculous. You're not an alcoholic," Duane told Robert. If Robert's an alcoholic, then he wouldn't be able to hang out at the bar with Duane. If Robert is an alcoholic, and Duane drinks more than Robert, then what does that make Duane? Duane could tell Robert stories about real alcoholics—mean, nasty drunks, a trope unto themselves. People who ended up dead or in jail because of their drinking—now that was the definition of an alcoholic that everyone could agree on.

But what about alcohol abuse, or dependence? Can you routinely drink too much without being an alcoholic? Can you stop? A counselor we saw said, "The hardest thing for an alcoholic to do is have just one drink a night. If you can do that for a year, then you're probably okay." He was talking to me.

My definition was: if it changed your behavior in a negative way, I don't care what you call it, it has to stop. My own relationship to alcohol changed when I got pregnant with our first child. I went from being a reliable accomplice, keeping Robert company drink for drink, to "no fun." After McCullough was born, I was nursing her and wasn't interested in drinking. Being the one who got up in the middle of the night and first thing in the morning meant I wasn't interested in staying up late or waking up with a headache. That didn't mean I stopped drinking completely. And as McCullough grew older and after Jack was born, it didn't mean that I never over imbibed, but I didn't *need* to drink.

When the cycle of Robert's on-again, off-again drinking and the inevitable arguments reached an unbearable pitch, a friend of mine suggested we go see Billy, a marriage therapist, who specialized in alcoholism. He was a recovering alcoholic himself. There was nothing, he told us, that he didn't know about alcoholics and alcoholism. During one of our first sessions Billy said to Robert, "You're either an asshole or an alcoholic. Which one do you want to be?" "He's both," I said.

"No, Tara. It's one or the other. An alcoholic might do asshole-like things, but it's a disease, and if you accept that, then you can't have it both ways, any more than Robert can." Robert didn't think he was either one. He thought the biggest problem with his behavior was that I was "too sensitive."

Another thing Billy told us frequently: "It's a *family* disease." I thought we were in his office so he could help me set Robert straight. Suddenly, the tables were turning. He turned his kind blue eyes on me and suggested that I might benefit from taking a look at myself. I couldn't understand what he was talking about: I was the one who took care of the house, took care of the kids, and held down a job. I was the one who kept to our budget and didn't overspend. I was the one who time and again agreed to whatever scheme Robert had come up with because he insisted it would make him happy. How was anything wrong in our marriage my fault?

Billy told me I should be going to Al-Anon. I'd heard of it of course. It's a support group for the family and friends of alcoholics. Caught in the throes of terrible dysfunction it's good to hear people tell stories that help you say to yourself, "I know! Robert does that too." But when Billy brought it up, I wasn't interested. I wasn't the one with the drinking problem or the bad behavior. "It would help you understand that you're not alone," he said. He pointed out that my list of grievances, resentments, and bruised feelings were poisoning me as much as I thought Robert was. That I was becoming, had become combative and judgmental. It made me crazy to hear that I had to do so much work to understand and offset Robert's behavior.

"Smile. Laugh it off, "Billy said. "Make a joke out of it. Don't take everything Robert says and does so seriously." There were too many times when that seemed impossible.

Billy kept talking about Al-Anon. And I kept resisting. I didn't have the time. Or more accurately, didn't want to spend any more time thinking or talking about Robert. He was already consuming my life. I didn't want to give over any more of it to him. Then Billy told me about Caron, a rehab center in Pennsylvania that also ran programs for the family members of alcoholics. He encouraged me to sign up.

Why would I want to go to a weeklong therapy session in the middle of nowhere, when I flatly refused to go to an hourlong meeting in a room a couple of blocks from our apartment? Maybe it was the prospect of getting away from Robert for a week. He would get to juggle the kids, the house, and his job. My role. A role he didn't seem to value. Maybe it was my competitive nature saying, "Recovery? I'll show you how to do recovery."

About a month or so later I was driving up a long, paved road, in a semirural town to a cluster of brick buildings that would be my home for the next week. The program was meant to get us, a group of nine adults of mixed ages, sexes, and backgrounds, to strip away our defenses and coping mechanisms and face our own behavior. We weren't allowed to bring books; there were no TVs. Cell phones and iPads didn't exist yet. The only exercise allowed was a walk around the campus. We were taught to see the many ways that alcohol permeated our lives and shaped our responses, reactions, and assumptions; to recognize our anger, and resentments. Every one of us in the group had an active alcoholic in our life, and that was what brought us to Caron. But we didn't focus on them. We started with our families of origin.

It was not news to me that alcohol was part of my culture. I could easily say that my mother's father, Grandfather Sullivan, was an alcoholic. My mother told me that. So did my grandmother, Grandmere. There were stories. He would disappear for days at a time. He would return home without his overcoat or his watch. "He'd misplaced them." "He'd given them away." But he was kind, gentle, loving. It wasn't a problem. *He* wasn't a problem.

As I learned to decipher the code that each family develops to tell their stories and acknowledge uncomfortable truths, I saw the dynamic shift. The alcoholic creates chaos, which is its own dysfunction, but those around the alcoholic often overcompensate in trying to control the chaos and the alcoholic and in the process create a rigid set of rules. High expectations of everyone else. This was Grandmere. She ran a tight ship. Gave the marching orders. She organized everyone and everything around her. She was loving if you were in agreement. She was blistering if you crossed her. *I* was Grandmere.

In those seven days I hardly talked about Robert at all. When Billy said, "Alcoholism is a family disease," it had two meanings. Alcoholism is genetic and often passes from generation to generation. And alcoholism affects the whole family regardless of who is or isn't drinking. Neither of my parents drank much. I don't remember my father drinking at all. His mother, my Grandmother Helen, drank and smoked, even though she was tethered to an oxygen tank because of her emphysema. Years after she died, I was introduced to the plays of Tennessee Williams and I instantly thought of her; she could have stood in for any of his fragile, hysterical, alcohol-dependent heroines.

Both my parents had families they wanted to get away from, but I doubt they understood that alcoholism might have been an underlying reason why. Alcoholics Anonymous was founded in 1939. Al-Anon in 1951. My parents married in 1955. My mother had just recently turned twenty. Though Grandmere told me in a confessional moment that my grandfather "went to a couple of AA meetings," in their world and culture drinking problems were the norm, to be dealt with behind closed doors. Self-help groups were unknown. Confession was something one did on Saturday in the safety of the church. Not in public. At any rate, Bill Sullivan died in 1959, and I'm quite sure that from Grandmere's point of view, the problem of alcohol died with him. Of course, it hadn't. It forged her judgments on how life was to be lived. She continued to impose her standards of behavior on her children long after they'd left home. Her criticisms could be withering. Her self-righteousness unassailable. She passed this bundle of rules and judgments on to my mother.

My mother, who broke away from her family's norms and expectations to marry a man who similarly rejected his family's code of behavior, was still susceptible to her childhood conditioning. She unknowingly carried Grandmere's bundle with her. My mother's criticisms could also be withering and her self-righteousness unassailable.

Even as a child, I sensed this. The judgmental tone, the cutting remark, and sharp edge of the usually soft voice—my mother could sound very much like her mother. At Caron, I came to learn that this phenomenon was as real a thing as the red hair and blue eyes passing through our generations. And that my mother had passed this same bundle on to me. I'd inherited, and integrated into my behavior, an entire history of dysfunctional thinking. And I'd prided myself on being the well-adjusted one.

In one of our group sessions we learned how children in dysfunctional families cope by unconsciously taking on roles that help them navigate the sense of uncertainty in their lives. My parents married young and in four years had five children. Brian, Maura, me, and the twins, Sarah and Justin. A couple of years later, my mother delivered a boy two months premature. She was never clear on whether he was stillborn or died after birth. And then a year after that my youngest sister, Ursula, was born. My parents were ill-equipped, emotionally and financially, for such an onslaught of children.

No surprise, then, that Brian, the oldest of my brothers and sisters, stepped into the role of Hero. He assumed the man-of-the-family role early on. By the time he was in first grade he would get up in the morning, throw a few logs into the wood-burning furnace in the basement, go out to the barn to milk our cow, Ophelia, a fawn-colored Guernsey, and return with the milk pail in time to make oatmeal for everyone before school.

My older sister Maura was, after my parents separated, easily identifiable as the Rebel. She was the one who dared to talk back to the nuns at school. She was the one who yelled, "Fuck you!" to the principal, Sister Anne, as I sat mutely terrified in the outer office. I froze when she flung open the door and stormed out, saying, "C'mon. We're going." I looked back at Sister Anne, fearful and ashamed, as speechless as the nun. The repercussions for Maura were immediate. She was expelled from school. Consultations with a psychiatrist followed. Medication prescribed. Nonconformity would not be tolerated.

Sarah was the Lost Child. Sarah, who at age four had both her legs broken when she was head-butted by a ram in the pasture. She lay alone in a hospital room for weeks with her legs in traction, my mother and father too busy with chores, work, and four other children to visit regularly. She's said that much of her childhood is a black hole, and she's fine with that. She's the most balanced of all of us, so she's going to leave well enough alone.

Sarah's twin, Justin, was equally lost but assumed the role of the Mascot or Clown. Freckled and feckless, his high energy and goofiness either amused us or got him into trouble. Justin spilled his glass of milk all over the dinner table, the white liquid flowing under the placemats, dripping down the legs of the table, soaking the paper napkins we threw at it to clean up the mess. "I knew you were going to do that," my mother said, as my father sat stone-faced at the head of the table. "Well, why didn't you tell me?" Justin cried.

The baby of the family, Ursula, was, well, the baby. I have a memory of her at six years old—blonde, blue-eyed, and seemingly angelic—after we moved in with my grandfather in Providence, standing outside the house one afternoon screaming a stream of obscenities that she'd picked up from the kids at the local grammar school. I don't know what set her off, only that I was simultaneously in awe and terrorized.

And me, the middle child. The people pleaser. I did it as a kid. I would do it as a wife. As children we all had assigned chores, but I took pleasure in doing them before I was asked or reminded. I would come home from school and set the table for dinner. I would do the laundry. Iron my grandfather's boxer shorts. I babysat and had a paper route by the age of twelve, all I suppose, to prove how responsible I was. The respecter of authority and rules. If you play by the rules, then everything will be okay. If you don't, criticism would be the least of it.

I was the observer, the mental recorder, of all that was going on. But seeing it is not the same as being able to change it. And sometimes seeing it is also not the same as knowing what it really means, particularly when alcoholism and family dysfunction are involved.

I sat in the living room when I was twelve pretending to read a book as I listened to my mother on the phone with Grandmere. From the one-sided conversation I could glean that my mother was defending herself for having so many children. Children that as far as I could tell she had only because in an odd adherence to her Catholic faith (which she had all but given up) my parents never used birth control, except the clearly unreliable rhythm method. Similarly, I understood on a visceral level that my father was having an affair with his secretary in the English department when one day after picking me up from school he said, "I just have to stop by a friend's apartment and pick up a book." I wonder why he let me follow him into the apartment. The friend, Alice, was not home, but the book was on the bedside table.

Everything I learned that week at Caron took years of repetition in therapy and Al-Anon meetings to really understand. And still longer to integrate.

Robert would go to Caron a few years later, after he'd started drinking again, more than before and with no apology or restraint. Calls to the patient were not allowed as many of the program attendees had chaotic and unsupportive home environments. Families were encouraged to come visit on campus. I missed him. I made the long drive to this now-familiar place. It was midway through his monthlong program. I brought him a photo album that I'd put together: All the People Who Love You, Miss You, and Want You to Get Better. Photos of our children, our friends, our charmed life. Evidence of how much he had and how much he had to lose.

I attended an AA meeting with Robert during that visit. One after another, people stood up and spoke of their gratitude for their family's love and support, and their gratitude for their sobriety. Robert didn't speak, but I saw him sharing the photo album with the people he'd become close to during his stay. What was he telling them? This is who I really am? This is who I want you to see when you see me?

PARK SLOPE, BROOKLYN, 1998.

Robert's aunt died a few months ago. He always knew there would be more inheritance coming his way. We're stunned to find out how well she'd invested. Practically as soon as Robert hung up the phone with the bank, he started to plan his future.

On the list: A Ferrari Dino in Switzerland.

"It says here it's in mint condition. You know it doesn't cost that much to fly a car overseas. And the prices are better there. It's practically a wash."

"You're going to buy a car without driving it? Just wire the money—sight unseen?"

A picnic boat.

"I hear Sirius might be up for sale. You know I've always intended to have a picnic boat, so we could do some overnight cruising. And Raven's wet. The picnic boat would have a head. You'd like that."

"Think about the amount of wood on a boat like Sirius. You know how much it costs just to wood Raven. It would be insane. And I'm not going to do it!"

Now we could have the house in Maine with a deep-water dock.

"The house on Greenings? We should go see it this summer."

"Robert, they want a couple million for that house. There's nothing wrong with Connor Point. It's a really sweet spot. It's uncomplicated. We don't need a deep-water dock."

"Well, maybe we should hold on to it. Have both. We can use Connor Point as a rental."

A restaurant.

He could be a chef/owner like his former boss, David Waltuck, at Chanterelle. He wouldn't have to bother with investors.

"The problem with investors is they take all the profit."

"The advantage to investors is that they share the risk!"

"This is my dream. I've always wanted to have a restaurant. After working at Chanterelle and Bolo, I know how to do it."

"There's a big difference between working in a restaurant and being the chef/owner. You have to be there all the time. That means no going away to Maine in the summer."

"It will be slow in the summer. I can get away for a few long weekends."

He wanted to follow the Chanterelle model: elegant haute cuisine. The flatware would be silverplate, the dinnerware would be fine china, the glassware would complement the wines. Linen tablecloths and napkins, of course. Candesticks with silk shades on the tables. Wallpaper with gold foil squares and upholstered red banquettes. It would be a special-occasion restaurant in a neighborhood of delis, take-out, and faux Mexican with a noisy bar scene fueled mainly by beer and margaritas.

"Didn't you tell me that eighty five percent of new restaurants fail in the first year?"

Any argument against it only convinced Robert that I wasn't supportive. My misgivings were a lack of faith in him. I was standing in the way of his dream.

"This is what the inheritance is for. I'm not buying the car from Switzerland!"

There would be no investors. He wasn't going to budge on that point. He was having a hard enough time discussing or justifying his decisions with me. He didn't want to answer to investors, but he didn't want to do it alone either. Despite dismissing my opinions when they didn't align with his, he wanted me there to help him. He could rely on me to train the staff, to be the friendly face at the door, to recognize our friends who traveled over from Manhattan, to manage the myriad number of small details, to step in when the dishwasher didn't show—all so he could focus on cooking.

We loved the 1996 movie *Big Night* about two Italian brothers on the Jersey Shore struggling to make a go with their authentic Italian restaurant. They suffer through many nights of no customers, or the few they have being displeased with the menu. It's a warning that being enamored of food and being a great cook aren't the only ingredients needed for success. In the iconic final scene, one of the brothers comes into the kitchen after a disastrous night and, without speaking, makes a simple omelet, then shares it with the waiter and his brother. It can be seen as a eulogy for their business, or an ode to the essence of eating, or as a new beginning. Robert and I always saw it as a new beginning. I suspect Robert saw himself as Primo, the chef brother, and me as Secondo, the manager brother. But maybe when movies are your points of reference for how to succeed, or how not to fail in business, your thinking isn't grounded in reality.

Robert had already had two careers. He'd been a photographer and taught photography at Muhlenberg College in Allentown, Pennsylvania, and he was working as an architect when he decided to go to night school for cooking. He loved to cook. No one ever turned down a dinner invitation when he was cooking. He made dining out a study of food and wine. He went to Paris when he was sixteen with classmates and ate at La Tour d'Argent. Our second trip to Paris was in essence a culinary tour from bistros to the haute of haute cuisine, the sort of places that you had to book six weeks out to get a table. I didn't have Robert's stamina or digestive system and begged off the last lunch, when I simply couldn't imagine swallowing another mouthful of butterfat. I told him, afraid that he would get mad that I was spoiling his plans, but he admitted that he too had had enough. At Chanterelle in New York, he'd gone from being a regular customer to interning in the kitchen to being hired as a line cook. He felt that he was ready to take on, if not New York City as a whole, at least our neighborhood in Brooklyn.

He had high hopes for recognition in the New York food world. But at that time Park Slope was not known for its cuisine. Of course, he hoped to be reviewed in the *New York Times*. When you dream big, you dream of big success too. He did get reviewed but not in the

Times. And not until he shifted course and turned Vaux (a nod to architect and landscape designer Calvert Vaux—and confusing to pronounce, vox) into Vaux Bistro.

New York magazine featured Vaux Bistro with a photo of Robert (close-cropped hair, white chef's jacket) in its Underground Gourmet column:

> Vaux Populi
> It used to be that hard-to-please Brooklynites would venture all the way into "the city" seeking culinary excellence (or just a decent steak-frites). Nowadays, in newly chef-infested areas like Boerum Hill and Williamsburg, the only question is how much they'll pay when they stay in the neighborhood. Robert Willis (pictured), one of the brave new breed of Brooklyn chef-owners, found out the hard way. After stints at Chanterelle and Bolo, he opened Vaux in Park Slope last December with grander aspirations and higher prices than had been seen thus far on Cucina boulevard (that stretch of Fifth Avenue renamed for its haute-pasta pioneer), but despite great reviews and Saturday crowds, Willis couldn't sustain weekday business with entrees pushing 30 bucks. So last week, after painting the façade bright red and hanging mirrors above the comfortable

banquettes, Willis reopened the erstwhile New American Vaux as the pared-down gentler-priced Vaux Bistro. Now the menu reads rustic French, with daily specials like coq au vin, beef stew and bouillabaisse ($16 each), and more wines in the $20-to-$34 range, soon to include the best of each Beaujolais cru, selected by celebrity sommelier (and neighbor) Daniel Johnnes. What makes a bistro a bistro? In Vaux's case, a well-dressed frisee salad with meaty lardons and hot garlic croutons, an atypically unpureed leek-and-potato soup, a house terrine de canard, creamy steamed mussels. If the splendidly moist duck in watercress sauce wasn't so good, you'd order it for the first-rate frites alone. And with a $10 pasta du jour supplanting the $20 lobster risotto, Vaux Bistro has family-restaurant potential. At least it seemed that way on reopening night, with a lively infant captivating a window table and a toddler asleep on a banquette—fortunately for his mother, within carrying distance of home.

The reviewer was right about one thing: Vaux Bistro was family friendly. Many nights Jack, McCullough, Nora (a German exchange student who lived with us for a year), and I would have dinner at Vaux Bistro before heading home to do homework. Sometimes it seemed that

Vaux was just an extension of our kitchen. We held Thanksgiving and Christmas dinners there, pulling all the tables together to form one long table down the center of the room, our family and friends filling the restaurant in lieu of customers.

Robert could work incredibly hard. I knew that. What I questioned was his staying power. His interests changed frequently. I didn't doubt that he could create a beautiful place, that he could cook wonderful food, that people would want to come and be a part of it. But how long would it last? How long before he wanted to be off doing something else? How long before the inevitable problems that plague restaurants surfaced? I knew many of them from years waitressing: finding good people to work with and then keeping them happy, staff shortages, no-shows, problems with deliveries, deathly slow evenings in the middle of winter. Robert's temperament didn't seem suited to the challenges of running a restaurant long-term, and I was decidedly uninterested. It wasn't my dream. But I did it anyway. Maybe I was part of the problem. If Robert had a business partner who was as enthusiastic as he was, not a reluctant conscript, he would have had someone who could truly share the workload and responsibility. I wasn't that.

I wake up when Robert slides into bed at three a.m. It's not the movement that rouses me; there's a sour stink in the air. The smell of alcohol not on the breath but seeping through the pores of his skin. It's the smell of sickness, a slow death, failure. Feigning sleep, I turn away. I know better than to tell an alcoholic who's drunk that they're in denial. It will wait.

I'd said it was insane for him to open a restaurant. A fancy restaurant with an expensive wine list and an elegant bar. It's difficult enough for an alcoholic to work in a restaurant kitchen: after-shift camaraderie often includes a drink on the house and nothing to stop you from buying more. But it's also possible to say goodbye, walk out the door at the end of the night, relying on the strength of the program and taking it one day at a time. It's quite another to be the chef/owner responsible for every element, chief among them, sampling wines, searching for the best to compliment his menu. As owner, you are often the last one out the door. There's cleanup to supervise, inventory to be done for the next day's order, receipts to be tallied, often while sitting at that elegant bar, facing an enticing array of camaraderie in a bottle.

I'd said it was suicide. He said I didn't trust him. Do you trust yourself? I asked. Of course, he said. I said I didn't think it was a test he needed to take. He said he knew plenty of people from the program who worked in restaurants; they didn't drink. I couldn't prove or disprove that. He might not have my trust, but he demanded my faith. Do it with me, and then you'll see. You'll be there. It was a lifelong dream, he said. If I don't do it now, who knows if it will ever happen.

The discussion had moved from the threat to his sobriety to the what, where, when, and how to do it. My freelance job as a writer and producer in the marketing department of Lifetime Television meant that I often worked at night when studio time was most available. It was a job I loved, and I was bringing in more salary than Robert. But the inheritance meant I could quit my job and take care of the kids, he said. And help with the restaurant, he added. I had plenty of experience. When Robert met me I was waitressing at a trendy place on the Upper West Side. It was only the latest in a long list of restaurants I'd done time in. I had wanted it to be my last. Robert was persuasive, and persistent. He knew instinctively how to enlist me. The carrot and the stick. The reward of making him happy, the challenge of proving that I was capable.

Now, less than a year since we opened Vaux, a twelve-minute walk from our brownstone, Robert was drinking again. Now, he had not just his wife and family counting on his sobriety, but the fate of a new business, and a staff that needed to be managed and paid. As I woke up to get the kids ready for school, I looked over at Robert. His back was to me, but I could still smell the alcohol. Should I be grateful that at least he came home last night? Was that evidence of some sense of responsibility on his part? I had little interest anymore in seeing his point of view, or in trying to find a middle ground. We had a deal. Disease or no disease. When did he start up again? Was he going to meetings and drinking? Or had he stopped going to meetings altogether? Who else knew? Robert's sobriety wasn't a secret. Were any of my friends at the restaurant covering for him? Was he downing shots of vodka after everyone else left for the night? Or was he treating the staff to multiple rounds after their shift, buying their complicity in his own downfall? Because downfall was how I saw it.

I made lunch for Jack and McCullough. Got them ready for school. Grabbed the leashes. It was my routine to bring the dogs, my little Scotties, and after I took the children to school, go to Starbucks for a latté. I was trying to pretend that nothing was wrong, but I doubt my anger at Robert was masked by my false cheer. I left a note for him: "Walking the dogs after drop-off. Be back by 9:30. T." I didn't add my usual XXOO.

When I got back, Robert was in the kitchen making coffee. "What?" he said. He looked at me warily. I briefly wondered how he was feeling. Did he have a headache? Was his stomach in turmoil? His eyes looked puffy and still a little glazed. I took a long slow breath, even as I was twisting the dog leashes around in my hands. In the past hour walking around our neighborhood, I hadn't worked out what I was going to say. My anger felt venomous. Historical. I was one of a long line of long-suffering self-righteous Kelly-Sullivan-Murphy women. Anger stoked by resentment by what was happening to me. By what Robert was putting me through.

I tossed the leashes on the counter and saw Robert flinch at the noise. Something shifted then. I was done fighting. I wasn't going to shout, berate, accuse.

"Robert," I was calm. "I can't keep you from drinking. But I'm not going to be married to you if you do. It's your choice." He didn't pretend not to know what I was talking about or deny it.

"That's not a choice. You don't have the right to tell me what to do."

"I'm not telling you what to do. I'm telling you what I'm going to do." I was finally putting myself first and not apologizing for it. "Your actions have consequences. This is one of them. It's rehab or divorce. It's entirely your choice."

Despite everything I knew about alcoholism, and my belief and acceptance that it was a disease, it was still hard not to think that Robert was simply being willful. When he defended his right to drink despite the damage it did to our relationship, our marriage, our family, our bank account, it made me livid. He was a smart man. He'd already been to rehab once. I'd assumed that he would be like a kid who'd been caught stealing. He'd say, Oops. Guess you caught me. Sorry. I'll try to do better. Even, It's a disease. Or, I need help.

But there was none of that. No apology. Instead, he was the one berating and accusing. He wasn't ready to give it up. But he finally agreed to go. Neither of us happy. He felt forced. I didn't like being the enforcer. We were wearing each other out.

MAINE—THE WAY LIFE IS

GREENINGS 1998

Robert bought and sold real estate on Mount Desert with regularity, trying out different locations, taking in different views, always evaluating everything by its access to the water. We'd sold the two-bedroom cottage in Bernard during one of Robert's cash-flow squeezes and had been happily renting a series of summer rentals. Then a charming carriage house came on the market. It was small but private and looked out over a cove. Best of all, it was low maintenance. Close it up at the end of summer; don't think about it until the following June. For a couple of years Robert was content; then one of his aunts died. The inheritance he'd been counting on was far more than he'd been expecting, and suddenly the little cottage on Connor Point wasn't good enough. Robert aspired to a deep-water dock, where he could tie up *Raven,* with no need to row out to the mooring.

We spent a lot of time at the Causeway Club, a small swimming and tennis club on the shore in Southwest. We met Kathy and her three red-headed children there at a barbecue. She was living on Greenings, a 100-acre island situated at the mouth of Somes Sound between Southwest and Northeast harbors, in a house her father, Jarvis, had bought to fix up and resell.

She was rowing back and forth from the island to Southwest. In fact, that was how she got here tonight, she said. It's only a mile, she assured me. Her father also owned a boat brokerage in town, so it was hard to imagine that there wasn't something with a motor that she could use. But as she described the house and island life, it became clear she was embracing living in another era. The house had no electricity and was lit by kerosene lanterns. The stove and refrigerator were powered by propane. She lugged her laundry over to town once a week. They had to chop wood for heat. There was no TV, no Internet, only a rotary-dial phone. It was as though she was describing Robert McCloskey's iconic children's book *One Morning in Maine*. She had a how-lucky-am-I? attitude.

"Which house is it?" we asked.

She pointed across the water to the shore of Greenings.

"You can just see it through the trees. You know it's for sale." We could barely make out a two-story shingle structure with a porch and two chimneys. We'd never noticed it before. Though the house was built very close to the water, it was screened from full view by a line of tall pines. As our children played together, we made plans to visit.

"You know, your boat *Raven* was built by the Thorpe family. Greenings Island was her first home."

We promised Kathy a ride in *Raven* in exchange for a tour of the house and island.

A few days later, Robert, the children, and I piled into *Raven* for our first visit to Greenings. A warm, sunny, clear day on the coast of Maine feels like a holiday, it's so rare. This was such a day, not a hint of fog in sight. The children wore only swimsuits. We left the harbor and turned up into the Sound. Five minutes later we pulled up alongside the dock. It was to be the first of many hundreds of such dockings.

The dock itself was a work of art: its walkway was supported by three enormous granite piers that already had withstood a centuries' worth of nor'easters and hurricanes. Those piers would probably stand for another hundred years. Looking over the edge of the dock we could see starfish lying on the ocean floor and clinging to the sides of the granite blocks. One year later we would stand on the dock on a warm summer's night and watch the noctilucae, millions of marine organisms, light up the water as our neighbor's boat pulled away in the dark.

Most of the Maine coast shoreline is granite outcroppings and rocks. Wherever a beach appears it is most likely not sand but covered with small rocks and pebbles. On Greenings, pools of water left by the receding tide filled granite bowls where snails and crabs scuttled to hide as the children's little hands reached to touch them.

In *One Morning in Maine,* a young girl, Sal, explores the seashore while her father readies the boat for a trip into Buck's Harbor. Sal's mother tends to the baby and preps for lunch in the kitchen of her old farmhouse. She stands in front of a porcelain sink and washboard peeling potatoes.

As we walked up the dock onto Greenings, and along the path toward the house, we felt as though we'd landed in the pages of McCloskey's book. Spindly pines with their twisted roots exposed held on with tenuous purchase to the rocky soil. Moss and ferns made up a multihued carpet of green under the pines. I imagined Sal there on the beach, holding a seagull feather.

At the head of the dock was a wood cabin, painted brown, with a small porch, and a dilapidated wood wheelbarrow just off the granite step. Kathy told us it was the captain's cabin. Inside tacked to one of the walls over the phone was a yellowed sheet of paper with a short list of phone numbers. It was so out of date it only listed the last four digits.

Kathy took us for a walk across the island to Sand Dollar beach. Most of the ten houses on the island were built quite close to the shoreline and had their own docks. There was no ferry service to the island. A rough dirt road wound around and through the center of the island connecting the houses by land, but there were only three vehicles on the island. A battered pickup truck that was shared by all the residents—used mainly for hauling firewood. One family had a small jeep, and there was an ancient but serviceable (so we were told) firetruck, retired to the island in case of emergency. It only took about twenty minutes to walk from one end of the island to the other.

As we stood in the field looking out past the farmhouse toward the Western Way, the family who lived there came out to greet us. Introductions were made. As I chatted with one of the older women, I marveled aloud, "This is so amazing. What an incredible view. I can't believe I've never been here before." She looked at me, not unkindly, and said, "Well, of course, you haven't. We don't know you." Greenings was privately owned. Invitation only.

The Thorpe family had settled the island in the 1800s, and local lore had it they were related to Henry Wadsworth Longfellow. The house Kathy was staying in had been built as a guest cottage in the 1930s for their grown children and grandchildren. The main house, Ravensthorpe, was a typical summer cottage—large, shingled, turreted with expansive wraparound porches, its shutters and doors painted inky black Seal Harbor green. It was hidden from view by a stand of pines. Ravensthorpe guests were expected to have dinner in the main house, so the guest cottage, the house where Kathy was staying, was only one room wide and was mostly bedrooms arranged around a large double-height living room.

We spent hours on Greenings that day. The house, the property, the view onto Somes Sound and the Claremont Hotel across the way, everything about it spoke to Robert. It reminded him of his grandfather's way of life. This was it, he said. He would never need anything more.

Yes, it was expensive, but really the only thing that mattered was his life in Maine. I too was enamored with the island, but I didn't entirely buy into the fantasy.

I stepped into my role as "The Responsible One":

- We can't afford it. It costs more than our brownstone in Brooklyn. And it's going to cost so much more in taxes than the cottage on Connor Point.
- We'll have to get electricity to it. Kathy might be happy rowing back and forth with a week's worth of laundry, but I'm not going to do that. We need to have a washer and dryer, to say nothing about lights!
- How am I going to get back and forth? I can't pilot Raven. What happens when you're not here? What if one of the children has an accident and I have to get them to a hospital?
- What about when things need to get repaired? How are they going to get out here? There's no ferry service to Greenings.
- And what about groceries?! All the other families on the island do a big once-a-week shopping. We're endlessly running into town for some item we've forgotten.

Robert had an answer for it all. We can afford it. Jarvis has arranged for a cable to run under water; we would only have to pay for getting the electric to the house, not from Southwest. Wasn't this the best way to spend the money he inherited from his family? Some of the other families use a local handyman with a boat to ferry them; we can hire Jeff too. Robert was sure that all the pluses would outweigh the negatives. I wasn't.

The house, which we would name Raven's Point, was built so close to the shore you could toss a rock into the water without leaving the porch. That was back in the day when the septic pipes from the house discharged directly into the ocean. Modern zoning didn't allow that, and the current building setback was 75 feet from the highwater line. Robert loved that the house was so close to the water's edge.

We bought it completely furnished. It was a time capsule from a long-ago era. There was a glass-fronted bookcase in the library that held decades of beach discoveries with little tags identifying the child who'd brought it home: barnacle cluster, found by Susan Wetherell, ten years old, July 1958. The cabinets in the pantry off the kitchen were filled with vintage green china and half a dozen different teapots. The linen closet held stacks of embroidered cotton pillowcases, and a cache of hot-water bottles still in their boxes, even a can of 1950s-era hairspray. The house stood patiently waiting to cast its spell on another small child who would walk its beaches and return with a treasure to store in the library bookcase.

The front porch looked north up the Sound and west. Summer sunsets turned the sky pink, flaming orange, and finally deep purple as the sun dropped below Flying Mountain. Some nights the sounds of a big band would waft over the water, coming from a party or wedding at the Claremont Hotel directly across the water. Several times a summer we would host large family dinners, and everyone would crowd onto the porch, sitting on the wide railings, sipping drinks and dipping into fresh crabmeat, passing the bug spray around to ward off the mosquitoes, the one blight, in an otherwise enchanted haven.

There were low-bush blueberries in front of the house and the children would pick them, eating as they foraged. McCullough found a large cranberry patch behind the cabin. Making cranberry sauce from the tiny berries became her end-of-summer ritual. We could hail a lobster boat from our dock and buy lobsters, just pulled from their traps, for dinner. We picked mussels off the rocks in front of the house at low tide. Jack would spend hours on the dock fishing for mackerel.

Those first summers at Greenings the children would spend much of the day playing around the rocks at the water's edge. I would sit on the porch reading a book and watch them as they explored what the tides washed up. As they got older and started sailing lessons, life on the water became a larger part of our life on Greenings. We bought two large rubber inflatables, powered by outboards. They were easier for me to handle than *Raven*. The boats could hold four or five people and boxes of groceries, but if the wind and tide were against us, we would get drenched as we negotiated the chop. The inflatables made it possible for me to stay on Greenings when Robert couldn't be there. One year, when Robert couldn't get time off from work, I'd spent much of the summer on Greenings alone with the children. After weeks of being marooned on the island because of fog, I'd purchased a compass for the inflatables. On a clear day, I made the trip each way, noting the compass settings. After that I could come and go regardless of the weather.

Every summer McCullough and Jack would each invite a friend from the city to stay on Greenings with us. When Jack was eight, he and his friend Lucio built a raft from the detritus of winter storms that washed up on the beach every spring: scrap wood, driftwood, and big chunks of Styrofoam that probably came from a destroyed float. The boys and McCullough paddled the raft, partially submerged, but still afloat almost all the way to the Claremont. Robert and I motored alongside in one of the inflatables, ready to rescue them if they capsized.

One summer's night in July, we took *Raven* and motored by moonlight over to Southwest and drove to Port in the Storm bookstore in Somesville, fifteen minutes away, to attend the first midnight sale of the latest Harry Potter book. McCullough and her friend Isabel would spend the next three days stretched out on the window seat in the stair hall reading their books cover to cover.

The property included a five-acre field that sloped down to the water's edge. Near the beach was an ancient tree with a swing. We placed a teak bench at the top of the field. The idyllic setting acted like a beacon for passing kayakers, who would drag their boats ashore and sit or wander for a while among the lupine and tall grass. These uninvited visitors rankled Robert, as he sat on his porch with the robin's egg blue ceiling and looked out at the world from his privileged perch.

"This is private property," he would fume. "They wouldn't like it if I pulled up to wherever they lived and picnicked on their lawn."

"You can hardly blame them. It's so beautiful. They're not bothering anyone—but you."

BOATS AND
BAD WEATHER

As the years of our marriage piled up, and the summers we spent in Maine accrued, I transformed into a seaworthy-enough sailor. More than that, I'd become a member of the community. I probably knew more people on Mount Desert than Robert did. When he came in the summers, he spent most of his time on the tennis court or on *Raven*. I'd discovered and made regular use of the hiking trails, carriage roads, and bike paths that crisscrossed Acadia National Park. I joined Friends of Acadia and helped with the annual fundraising auctions. Life as parent-in-charge meant I knew lots of other parents and their kids. I knew which unmarked road off Sargent Drive brought you down to the large, shingled cottage where Jack's friend Tyler's grandparents held their annual Fourth of July fireworks bash. I knew my way around the back roads by car and the marinas by boat.

So once again, when Robert's focus had turned to a new dream—he was opening a restaurant in Lakeville—he insisted I take the children to Greenings without him. He would come up whenever he could get away. Greg, a friend of Robert's, and a contractor, was already on the island doing repair work on the house. I wouldn't be totally alone.

It's hard to see the patterns and parallels of life when you're in the middle of living it. My summers on Greenings had become a rendition of my childhood summers on Prudence. I was in many ways as single as my mother and her sisters had been. Robert was absent a lot. Unlike me, my kids loved sailing and were good at it. McCullough was now one of the senior camp counselors at the sailing center. Jack, just a few years behind her, was a counselor-in-training. What I didn't see was how well equipped I'd become at navigating Robert's world—without him.

It was early in July and boat activity on the water was still light. The weather had been mixed for a few days. The fog hung off the Western Way threading its way into the harbor and then, like the tide, receding. After dinner it rolled back in, lacing the air with moisture so thick it sometimes felt like it was raining. The kids had taken one of the inflatables to Southwest. They were going to the movies in Bar Harbor.

On foggy days these expeditions always required a fair bit of negotiating amid quite a bit of angst on my part. They were competent sailors. They had their father's confidence when it came to boats and being on the water. But I knew that it didn't take much for something to go wrong. We agreed if it was foggy when they were ready to return to the island, they would spend the night at their cousin's house in Southwest.

McCullough had learned an early lesson in the hazards of boating one bright and sunny weekend afternoon when she was fifteen or sixteen. Not a shred of fog in sight. She was alone in the inflatable, speeding over to a friend's dock on the opposite shore, when the prop caught a submerged lobster pot line, bringing the boat to a violent halt and catapulting her into the frigid waters of the Sound.

Despite Robert's more relaxed attitude, before I agreed to let either of the kids pilot an inflatable by themselves, I'd insisted that they be able to climb into the boat from the water. It was harder than it might seem. The rubber sides were a good two feet high, and slippery when wet. They would practice by jumping off the dock, and even though the boat was tied up, it would scoot away as they tried to climb in. Once that was achieved, there were two absolute rules. Wear a life jacket, and clip the key to the outboard to the jacket. Then if you fall out of the boat, the key comes with you, instantly shutting off the motor. When she was thrown overboard, the motor stopped, the prop stopped, and the boat stopped. The thought of the damage a whirring prop could inflict on the human body was gruesome.

She was able to swim back to the boat and scramble back in. The worst thing from that episode turned out to be the loss of her favorite sunglasses. The best thing was that she wasn't hurt. But it was scary and sobering. Just growing up is a kind of survival. We are all tested in different ways and learn from those tests in different ways as well. Robert's many near-misses gave him a sense of invincibility and luck on his side. I think McCullough completely understood that she was going too fast and so did not see the submerged line, but she also knew that the basic safety rules she followed had saved her. Not all bad things happen in the dark. Sunny days are not safer days; we cannot see the accident before it happens, no matter how bright the sun.

After the kids left for Bar Harbor I went to bed early, book in hand. Sometime after I'd turned out the light, I heard shouting. It was indistinct but it was coming from the waterside of the house. I sat up, my pulse racing. The children had decided to come back in the fog and now they were in trouble! A few moments later there was an answering shout. Then silence. Then I heard it again. It was a man's voice. I couldn't tell if the person was drunk or in distress. But they were definitely on the water. I turned on my light and heard Greg open his door. I met him in the hallway.

"What's going on? Can you tell?" I asked him.

"I don't know," he said. "Sounds like someone's lost in the fog. Either that or someone's having a party on one of the boats."

The thing about fog, and water in general, is that sounds carry. The Claremont Hotel in Southwest Harbor, less than a half-mile across the channel from our house, was a popular venue for weddings in the summer. Many a night we had gone to sleep being serenaded by a band that sounded like it was next door. In the dark and the fog, it was hard to know where the voices were coming from.

"It doesn't sound like them, but it might be the kids." I ran downstairs, turning on lights as I went. I turned on the porch and dock lights and went outside. It was warm, and it wasn't raining. The lights looked like golden halos wrapped in a silver mist.

I peered into the darkness and called, "Who's out there?"

The man shouted again and this time I understood him. "Can you tell me where I am?"

"You're near Greenings, the northwest end, down from the farmhouse. Where are you trying to go?" I yelled back.

"I have to get to the Fleet," he said.

The Fleet was shorthand for the Northeast Harbor Yacht Club where the IODs (the International One Design racing fleet) were moored. It was around the corner, so to speak, but I would have said, on that night, "You can't get there from here."

I shouted to the man, "Follow the sound of my voice and I'll at least get you onto our dock, so you can get your bearings."

The route from house to dock ran along the shore. A grove of pine trees stood between the house and the captain's cabin at the head of the dock. The path followed the shoreline just a foot or so from the rocks leading to the water. To my right, the trees largely bare of lower branches stood like barely visible sentries, to my left the sound of an unseen ocean lapped quietly at the granite rocks on the beach. The shallow roots of the trees crisscrossed the dirt path of moss and pine needles. Long ago we'd installed path lights, some of which had gone out, and I felt my way carefully along. Greg, a reserved and taciturn man, followed silently behind me.

"Are you there? Can you hear me?" I called to the man in the boat.

"Ja," he said.

Moments later, as Greg and I walked down the ramp, I could just make out the silhouette of a rubber inflatable gliding up to the dock. We grabbed the line he threw, and Greg pulled him in, securing the boat on the bollard.

"I'm Jan," he said, introducing himself. "Thank you. I have to pick up some people at the Fleet and bring them out to *Rebecca*," he told us. *Rebecca*, a 139-foot sloop, was moored directly across the mouth of Somes Sound from our dock. "Where is the Fleet from here?" he asked.

Greg and I pointed into the blank darkness. There were no visible markers. "In that general direction. Do you have a compass?"

"Yes. But I've lost my bearings."

"I don't think it's going to happen," I said. "Maybe you can call them and tell them you'll get them in the morning."

"I have to get them, or I lose my job," he said. He was a new crewmember, from Norway or some other Scandinavian country, he didn't know the area, and his compass without coordinates was useless. It was nuts, I thought. I told him he could stay the night in the cabin. "Go in the morning," I said again.

"No, I have to pick them up." He moved to get back in his inflatable.

There's a passage in Beryl Markham's book *West with the Night* that resonates with me: "In any country almost empty of men, 'love thy neighbor' is less a pious injunction than a rule for survival. If you meet one in trouble, you stop—another time he may stop for you." That is how I felt about living on Greenings and about boating. Who knew when I would need someone's help? *Raven* lay alongside the dock. She had Loran, an onboard navigation system which gave depth readings as well as directionals. I looked at Greg. "What do you think? Are you up for an adventure?"

I would never have attempted it by myself, but Greg knew boats and knew how to pilot *Raven*. Greg didn't drink, but even better than that, he was sober-minded. He wouldn't say yes to doing something he wasn't comfortable with. Greg didn't show off.

I knew from those times with Robert that I would need to get up on the bow of the boat to be the lookout. I figured that together we might be able to lead Jan over to the Fleet, turn around, and find our way to *Rebecca* and then get back to Greenings.

"All right," Greg said.

Having the right equipment makes all the difference. We powered up *Raven* and turned on the Loran. A map of our area filled the screen in a glowing neon green light. As we slowly pulled away from the dock the little boat icon chugged across the screen moving away from the Greenings shoreline and in the direction of Northeast Harbor. I thought this must be what is feels like to fly through a cloud. With instruments for guidance, even though we couldn't see anything, we didn't feel like we were flying blind.

Jan followed us in his inflatable, staying just five feet off our stern. We motored slowly, throwing no wake, alert to a sudden hazard, but there was no anxiety. The Loran guided us into the Fleet, where a group of four people materialized on the dock. They greeted us with hearty shouts. We welcomed them onboard *Raven,* as it was the bigger boat, and then turned toward *Rebecca*. We made the trip over and back to our dock without incident, my confidence in Greg and the technology making me feel like an experienced boater.

When we got home, I called McC on her cell and told her to stay put in Southwest. We'd had enough excitement for one night.

"Not to worry, Mom. We're already at Katie's. We'll see you in the morning."

The next morning was clear, the fog having withdrawn as silently as it crept in. But as I woke to the cawing of the crows greeting the sun, I felt that I had vanquished not just the fog but my long-instilled fear of boats and bad weather.

Robert was willing to leave me in charge of the boats when he wasn't around. Was it because he recognized that I'd acquired some skill and confidence? Or was it, more likely, that he just didn't think about it, so immersed in whatever it was that he was doing. I don't remember his response when I told him the story of Greg's and my daring rescue. Politely complimentary would be my guess. But it didn't alter his basic perception that he knew what he was doing on the water, and I didn't.

Later that summer Robert was able to get away for a couple of weeks and come up to Greenings. One afternoon we ventured into Southwest Harbor. It was sunny, hot, and humid when we motored in from the island, but while we were in town, a gauzy fog blew in. On a clear day you can see all the way to Cranberry Island and Islesord. Now the islands were invisible. This was strange fog. Very white, very bright, but not dense. In a few places a boat's mast pierced the shroud, but the boat itself was undetectable. I suggested we return to town, visit with my sister for a while, and try later. Robert didn't want to wait.

Though the Coast Guard requires all boats to have life jackets, flares, and a foghorn, they aren't required to have navigation equipment. On this day, the compass was on the other inflatable.

"I've navigated worse at night," Robert said.

"Yeah, but you were in *Raven* and had the Loran. We don't even have a compass."

"All we have to do is point the boat in the general direction of the island. There's no way we can miss it. The worst that'll happen is we'll hit the shore and then we can cruise along to our dock. I can do it, okay? Why don't you just trust me?"

We cast off from the dock with Robert at the tiller, confident in his boating abilities. I sat opposite him to balance out the weight in the boat. Going from the marina through the harbor we could navigate from boat to boat. We passed *Mom's Mink* and *Black Fly,* working lobster boats. As we neared Beal's Wharf we saw that *Vagabond,* the charter fishing boat our twelve-year-old son was working on as a deckhand, was in her berth. We stayed as close to the shore as we dared after we passed the Coast Guard station, and then as we rounded the point, we needed to travel an imaginary line as if on a clock—going from seven to one.

It was so bright inside the fog it hurt our eyes. Creeping forward slowly, Robert told me to get far up in the bow to watch for buoys and other boats. "Sure, I'll go stick my neck out," I said. Every minute or so, I'd blast the airhorn. If an occupied boat was in the vicinity, it should answer. Oddly, there was not a sound. It felt to me as though the fog had swallowed the world.

Robert would kill the motor every few minutes to listen for a sign of where we might be. We couldn't hear a thing: no seagulls, no other boats, not even the water lapping on the shore. We couldn't see a thing, not boats moored at anchor, not the ghostly shape of a house, a dock, or a tree. We strained to see the large floats that the Hinckley boatyard stowed in the cove near our house. They didn't appear to exist.

It was less than a quarter of a mile from the harbor to our dock. But in that distance we got completely turned around. We had no idea where we were, in which direction we were headed, or where anything was. Robert was swearing.

"Shit. Fuck. I can't see a goddamn thing!"

I hated it when Robert swore. He'd refused to wait the fog out. He'd bullied me into going and now it seemed he couldn't handle it. He wasn't going to say, "Maybe we *should* have waited." It made me queasy.

"Listen!" Robert said. The sound seemed to come from the starboard aft side. There were only two bell buoys it could be. There was one marking the sandbar at the southwest end of Greenings and there was another at the mouth of Somes Sound. If we passed the bell buoy at the southwest end, we would be moving toward the Western Way. I imagined us floating out to sea. And yet I knew we couldn't be up by Somes Sound—we hadn't traveled far enough or long enough.

We inched forward. We weren't anywhere near the buoy, for suddenly in front of us we saw the farmhouse dock. Waves of relief washed over me. Robert smiled.

"See, I knew we'd be okay. Now we can follow the shoreline home," he said.

"No way. Let's tie up and walk home. We can come back later and get the boat."

"But we know where we are now. It'll be fine. Don't be so dramatic." Robert was confident again. But the fog hadn't lifted, and we would have to move offshore because of the shoals between the farmhouse and our dock.

"I've had enough. I'm getting out. You can do what you want, but I'm walking home."

Robert shrugged. "Suit yourself."

I stood on the farmhouse dock, watching him pull away, thinking, "I hope you do float out to sea."

DOGS

Despite most of a childhood spent in the country, I was never allowed to have a dog. "What practical purpose do they serve?" my father had asked. "A dog is just another mouth to feed." My answer would have been, if I knew how to put it into words, "A dog, *my* dog, will love me, will play with me, will always be happy to see me."

Instead, I made do with naming the pigs we raised, pretending they were pets—a relationship limited by the fact they were destined for the slaughterhouse. They were mostly black with streaks of white. With unintentional irony I called them Salt and Pepper. My desperation for a pet reached the level of the ridiculous when I brought home two hard-shell clams dug out of the sand from a trip to the beach. I put them in a glass bowl full of tap water on the desk in the small bedroom I shared with my sister. It took exactly one day for her to complain about the smell and two days for them to die.

So it surprised exactly no one when in my early twenties, after my brother Brian and I moved into a loft on the edge of Chinatown, that I got a dog. Not just any dog, but an Akita. An artist I worked for had one named Bill, who was devoted and loyal. A furniture dealer I knew had one, and his dog would go to the window and bark when he was down the block walking toward home. That was what I wanted. A dog that was so attuned to me it could hear my footsteps half a city block away. They had become the dog of the moment in early 1980s New York City. So popular that a store dedicated to only that breed, Akitas of Distinction, opened in the West Village and on the Upper West Side. But I didn't have the $1200 required for a brand-name puppy.

One day I saw an ad in the *New York Daily News* for Akitas. The breeder was a New York City cop. He lived in Queens. I took the subway out to a neighborhood of small two-story houses separated by chain link fences. The price was a more reasonable $400—just a few days' work on *All My Children,* where I had a regular gig as an extra. I brought my puppy home on the subway. I named him Chester.

He was a fawn-colored male with a black mask. The Akita tail is supposed to curl up and around in a tight spiral. His always unfurled, with a complete lack of distinction, making him look to a casual observer like a German Shepherd. Akitas had a reputation as fierce watchdogs, and I didn't mind that. As a woman in the city, I felt protected walking with Chester.

I took him with me everywhere. We would walk from the loft on White Street to the Spring Street Bookstore in SoHo. He would wait patiently tied up outside the store while I browsed for books, or hitched to a parking meter outside the Odeon while I had drinks with friends. Chester was with me the first time Robert and I met. We were sitting on the loading dock platform of 211 Restaurant having dinner with the owner, when Robert strolled by, came over to say hello to Khalil, and sat down.

Chester was the manifestation of my childhood desires. The missing element that would make me whole. I thought all he needed was love. Over the decades I would learn a lot about dogs, with each successive one giving me new insights, but poor Chester bore the brunt of my inexperience. He was housebroken and knew basic commands, but not much more than that. When I got him, I was often working jobs where he could come with me. We spent most of the day together. But when I had to leave him home alone, he was miserable. This was the beginning of his lifelong anxiety, which I didn't recognize for what it was and so never addressed.

In 1985, when I got Chester, the Internet didn't exist. Today a simple Google search about the breed reveals: "Akitas [were] bred as protectors, and bear-hunters. For centuries they were the companions to samurai. Akitas are a powerful, independent, and dominant breed, commonly aloof with strangers, but affectionate and deeply loyal with its family. A well-trained Akita should be accepting of nonthreatening strangers, otherwise they treat all strangers in an aggressive manner." And this, "Not for first-time dog owners."

I doubt I would have been dissuaded by these descriptions. In part because I desired loyalty and devotion, and in larger part because I didn't know what I didn't know. When he attacked my brother Justin, I didn't see it for it was. Even as I write that word *attack,* I realize I've never said it that way before. I always said *bit,* or *bite,* as though it were a minor thing. But in fact, Chester lunged at him, sinking his teeth into his forearm. Justin ran from the loft with blood pouring out of the five or six puncture wounds. He was hospitalized overnight so they could put him on an antibiotic IV drip.

"What happened?" everyone asked me.

As I told the story, I made excuses for Chester, and excuses for myself.

"I'd had the flu for a week. I really was so sick, I couldn't get out of bed. Justin was coming over and walking Chester for me. And then that morning, Chester refused to leave my side. He was growling at Justin. I was annoyed and grabbed his collar and then handed the leash to Justin, and Chester bit him."

I didn't know how to read my dog, or the situation. I was convinced his behavior was an aberration. An inexplicable, never-to-be-repeated event. There were no more biting incidents, though he did growl. Perfectly reasonable, I would think. Chester is warning the person. So much better than a surprise attack. I was mildly aware that some people were scared of him, but I thought that's because they don't know him like I do. Chester accepted Robert in my life, and Robert wasn't put off by Chester, so I never had to choose between them.

Stories began to accumulate. I was working for an independent filmmaker, in the neighborhood, when I was called to the phone.

"Tara, it's Scott. I think Chester's on the ledge outside Robert's apartment." Scott was the friend at our wedding who wondered if we'd make it to five years.

"What are you talking about? He can't be!"

"Well, there's a big dog out there, and I think it's the tenth floor. Isn't that your apartment?"

Robert's loft was in an 1860s-era building with an eighteen-inch-wide cornice below our window. It wrapped around the two sides of the building that faced the streets.

I dropped the phone and ran the two blocks home. When I arrived, our front door had been broken in, but the action was next door at my neighbor Steve's apartment. It was teeming with men: the NYC Fire Department, animal control officers from the SPCA, friends from the neighborhood, and a few people I didn't recognize, perhaps the type that gravitate to a drama with a potentially awful ending. A fireman outfitted in a harness and secured to a large column in the apartment was getting ready to crawl out and capture Chester, after he had been shot with a tranquilizer dart. To my, and I'm sure the rescuer's relief, Chester chose this moment to walk back in. Did he hear my voice? Did he sense that I had returned? *The News of the World* got hold of the story and ran it with this headline: "The Ledge of Barkness! Soap actress stars in her own real-life drama!"

"What happened?" everyone asked me.

I couldn't really say. What I did know was that a window in our apartment was open, and Chester managed to crawl up and out and then walk along the ledge without falling off until he came to the end of the building. Somehow, he managed to turn himself around, and then he came inside.

Unequipped to understand what was happening, unable to explain why Chester was behaving the way he did, I wrote every episode off as a fluke and went on as before. Now I know that Chester wasn't crazy. He was following his instinct. His life's purpose, his reason for being was to be with me, and he would go to extraordinary lengths to make that happen.

"What happened to the side of the barn?" Robert asked me. We were now living in Maine in a rental. It was the winter I was wooding *Raven*. For some reason I couldn't take Chester with me to the boatyard that day and didn't want to leave him cooped up inside, so I clipped him on the dog run, which had worked before. While I was gone, he gnawed about four feet of clapboards on the corner into splinters, trying to free himself.

"That will be expensive to repair," Robert said.

"I'll take him with me next time I go to the boatyard," I promised.

"You'll never believe what happened," I said to Robert a couple of days later.

This time it was the Volvo. I'd taken Chester to the boatyard with me, as I said I would, but decided when I got there that he'd be more comfortable in the car. When I came out an hour or so later to check on him, I discovered he'd completely shredded the interior, from the dashboard to the rear compartment. The moment I opened the car door he greeted me with joy and a wagging tail. No sense on Chester's part that he'd done anything wrong, just pleased to see me.

He'd done this not because he was destructive. Not because he was bored. He was trying to get out because he was supposed to be with me. But of course, that's not what it looked like to me or Robert. To us it looked like I had a dog who was losing his mind. Friends recommended a vet outside of Ellsworth who might be able to help. I wasn't sure what he could do, but I made an appointment, describing the car, the barn, numerous other episodes. When I arrived, they asked me to muzzle him. The vet was afraid to touch him.

That was when I made the decision to put Chester down. I couldn't give him what he needed, which seemed to be 24/7 access to me, and I couldn't turn him over to someone else's care knowing how destructive he could be in his attempts to get back to me. I left him with the vet who was afraid to touch him without a muzzle on. I knew I'd failed him over his lifetime, and I knew I was failing him in the moment he needed me most, to comfort him on his way out of this world. To honor his commitment to me by staying by his side. The remorse I felt as I walked out the door has never completely left me.

I took a break then from dog ownership, and Robert breathed a sigh of relief. But my image of myself includes a dog by my side. I bought books and magazines dedicated to particular breeds. Retrievers. Terriers. Poodles. I would spot an unusual dog—"Look, there's a Briard!"—the same way Robert spotted cars we passed on the road. "Look, there's a GTC." Robert gamely accompanied me to breeders to check out their dogs.

A Giant Schnauzer. "Not a breed for a novice dog owner," the woman told us emphatically.

A Shar-Pei. "Just too ugly," Robert said.

A Mastiff. "In the city? Really, Tara?"

It wasn't long before I was determined to get another one, but I would learn from the mistakes I made with Chester. I chose an English bulldog puppy. She was everything Chester was not: small, uncomplicated, unthreatening. I named her Maude. She was funny, and sweet, and could clear a room with her gassy farts. She teethed on all McCullough's plastic toys. One day McCullough came to me in tears, holding the mangled remains of a stethoscope from a Play-Skool medical bag. "Now I'll never be a doctor," she sobbed.

We were still living in Maine but had decided to move back to New York. I was pregnant with Jack. I was having a hard time envisioning taking care of two children and a dog. Now it would be me walking Maude on a leash, navigating the city sidewalks pushing a baby carriage with a toddler in tow. Once again, I'd gotten a dog to fulfill the image of myself with a dog by my side. The problem was the image didn't square with my reality. Too busy. Too overwhelmed. Dealing with the specter of alcoholism, and constant moving. Feeling unmoored.

Somehow a dog was supposed to fix all that? My vet told me about a client who had two bulldogs. They might be interested in adopting her. They lived on the edge of town with a completely fenced-in yard. Their house was run-down, and they had terrible teeth, but their dogs were well cared for. I figured I knew how they spent their money. I gave them Maude and didn't look back. Was it the child in me that equated love and dogs without accounting for the love I needed to give in return?

For a while I was happily too busy to even think about dogs. If I did, it was with relief that I wasn't juggling another sentient being with needs. And yet a year or two later, feeling settled, with Jack out of diapers, the stroller almost a thing of the past, I started to notice dogs on the street again.

Then a friend who raised Scotties had a litter of puppies. A clean slate. I would do it right this time. Ellen wasn't so sure. "Scotties aren't great with kids. Jack might still be too young. They're a one-owner dog," she told me. She was reluctant, but by the end of the summer, when she still hadn't sold them all, she agreed to let me take one. Ellen told me to get a book, *The Art of Raising a Puppy* by the Monks of New Skete. These monks are a Benedictine order in upstate New York. Their life's work is the breeding and raising of German Shepherds. I was tempted to make a pilgrimage to see them but settled on reading the book and following it religiously. I worked with Roger. He loved learning. He loved the treats. He loved the attention. *I* was learning: to connect and communicate and actually create a relationship with my dog.

Roger was devoted to me, as Ellen had predicted, and he was good with McCullough and Jack, despite her fear that he wouldn't be. Walking Roger was my responsibility, but it was also my pleasure. "Going to walk Roger!" I would say, leaving Robert in charge of the kids after dinner. Roger loved to hike when we were in Maine. He loved the water. He loved boat rides on *Raven*. He made having a dog seem easy. Why couldn't I have left it at that?

Robert, *and* Roger, struggled to understand why one dog was not enough. Roger was perfectly happy as an only dog. Something that was made clear by his general disinterest in all those that followed. He never understood why I needed to have more than him. I couldn't explain it, to him, Robert, or myself.

A series of dogs took up brief residencies over the months that followed—flirtations that failed to fill the dog-shaped hole in my heart. It was as though I was scrolling through a dating app. Liking the look of this one or that one, inviting them in, trying them out, and then for one reason or another losing interest.

Harry, my friend Wendy's Border Terrier while she got settled across the country

Bruno, a boxer that only understood Russian and had bouts of diarrhea on our sisal rug

Diana, a Kerry Blue Terrier with a systemic skin condition

Spitty, my friend Wendy's second Border Terrier who needed a little training

Through my friend Ellen, I located a Scottish Terrier breeder not far from me on Long Island. It made sense to me to get another Scottie as I liked Roger so much. Marilee was serious about her breeding program and placement of her puppies. I was not allowed to choose the dog. Only that it be a female. She interviewed me. Lifestyle? How often did I walk Roger? And for how long? Did I have a securely fenced-in yard? Where would the dogs sleep? Crate training is a must! How many children did I have? What ages? Supervision is a must. Wait, are we talking about the kids or the dogs now? "And your husband?" "Well, he's mostly left this up to me," I hedged, "but he's supportive." Which meant, he knows I'm doing this despite his disinterest.

The first time I drove out to Marilee's in Huntington to meet my brand-new, picked-specially-for-me puppy, I didn't get to see any of the other dogs except the puppy's mother. Later, as Marilee and I became friendly, she let me meet the entire litter, but there was no second-guessing her choice. I'd fallen in love with my little brindle girl. I named her Francie. Sitting on the patio in the backyard of Marilee's 1950s Cape watching the puppies in the playpen, our conversations extended beyond dog care into confidences about our lives.

Robert had recently returned from his first rehab stay at Caron. Marilee was probably only ten years older than I, but she seemed much older, maybe because she was so different. She was conservative, contained, and coifed. Her husband was retired military. Army? Marines? A distinction I didn't focus on. Childless. Or did they have a son who was estranged from them? I can't remember. Breeding and showing Scotties was what sustained her. She was curious about Caron. About alcoholism. The intensity of her interest unnerved me. I was still feeling my own way, still learning a new language for describing the dysfunction I was enmeshed in. I sensed she was living in a cocoon she had spun for herself. She was ready to break out, but I wasn't up to the task of being her guide. I was having a hard enough time navigating for myself. After I took Francie home, I gradually let the friendship lapse, letting greeting cards go unanswered. The connection I was looking for was on four legs, not two. I still didn't recognize that my dogs needed something from me as well; it wasn't supposed to be a one-way relationship.

Which is why, after we moved to Lakeville, Connecticut, I figured life in the country gave me license to have more dogs. Over the years I acquired:

Rocket, a Pitbull mix with a limp who we rescued from a horse barn

Milo, a Miniature Wire-Haired Dachshund instead of the cat that McCullough really wanted

Homer, a yellow Labrador Retriever from a litter that my neighbor had

When the number climbed to five, it began to register with me that the dogs weren't providing the solace and companionship that were the underlying reasons for having them in the first place. They were a pack, and I was the leader, but the moments of individual connection were few. We'd moved to a smaller house. It was impossible to police them from getting on the furniture or being underfoot in the kitchen. They were relegated to the mudroom, with a dog door, so they could come and go at will. They were background, part of the fabric of my life. The image of me with a dog by my side had been negated by the sheer number of them. I was beginning to see that the need was something like an addiction and that it was making my life unmanageable.

Sometimes I wondered why Robert didn't stop me. Maybe he didn't try to stop me because he was collecting cars at the same rate I was acquiring dogs. Mostly, I felt that he wasn't very interested in what I did, only as much as it impacted him. Somehow, we were two adults, married for more than fourteen years, raising two children, sharing our daily lives, and yet in the most essential ways we were inaccessible to each other. There was an emotional chasm. We both wanted to be better understood by the other, but we had no idea how to get there. Therapy, rehab, yoga retreats, daily meetings, we'd tried them all and continued to, but some unnameable thing was eluding us. In the meantime, another dog or car would stand in for our inability to figure it out.

Robert came back from his last stay at Caron profoundly moved by a song they played in chapel at the end of his stay, "I Want to Know What Love Is" by Foreigner. He pulled it up on his phone, to share with me, tearing up as he listened:

> *I wanna know what love is*
> *I want you to show me*
> *I wanna feel what love is*
> *I know you can show me (hey)*

It was trite and sappy but I teared up too, saddened by Robert's naked need to be loved, and hurt by his inability to see that the woman sitting next to him on the couch wanted nothing more than to fill that need. I would never be able to. Robert's sense of loss and longing reached back to his birth. I think the song moved Robert to tears because he felt what he was missing and was reaching for it but wasn't unable to recognize it. But also, because he was the guy who cried at Hallmark commercials designed to pull at the heart strings. He had a misplaced pride in what he saw as his open emotions, because he was patently unwilling to experience vulnerability.

What I didn't recognize was that I was in a similar place as Robert. I had chosen to spend my life with a man who was unable to give or receive love, and I'd turned to dogs to fill that need. The idea that a thing will not fill the void within, the void created by lack of love or nurturing, is easy enough to understand. As a concept. We were living proof of the futility of that practice. It's easier to keep trying to fill the void with something new than to find peace within, or with each other. It's not that we didn't try, but always, just there at the edge of any moment, were the grievances.

MY DREAM

Within the year of Robert returning from rehab we were reconsidering our life in Brooklyn. The restaurant had successfully passed its one-year milestone, and while not wildly successful, it was holding its own. I sensed that the part of having a restaurant that Robert most enjoyed was the creation of it. The routine of running it, the ups and downs in reservations, inevitable staffing issues, and plumbing problems—these things were constants, and while Robert dealt with them, they chafed at his sense of independence. He didn't enjoy the day-to-day responsibilities, but the need for me to pitch in and help was now minimal.

My responsibilities were primarily taking care of McCullough and Jack, which was a pleasure. McCullough was taking riding lessons at Jamaica Bay Riding Academy off the Belt Parkway. We'd bought her a pony, and I was leasing a horse. Most afternoons we would drive out to the stable and ride. Jack wasn't interested in riding, but he was happy enough to come and hang out at the barn. We had two dogs. "We're living a country life in the city," I said.

I wasn't immune to the lure of other possibilities, fresh perspectives, redefining our lives. If Robert wasn't really committed to Vaux Bistro, I figured I might get ahead of the inevitable change and put my bid in. We both indulged in fantasizing about the luxury real estate in the back of the New York Times magazine. We saw a listing for a house in North Canaan, Connecticut. Likely not practical, but we called the broker anyway. It was an area we were somewhat familiar with, as several New York City friends had weekend houses in nearby Salisbury/Lakeville.

The idea that Tara and the kids and the dogs and the horses could live in the country while Robert would commute back and forth to the city for the restaurant wasn't realistic. Still, we went and looked. And in the way that sometimes decisions seem to present themselves, a neighboring business offered to buy Vaux Bistro. Shortly after that, Jack was diagnosed with dyslexia and we heard about a school, Kildonan, in Amenia, New York (a twenty-minute drive from Lakeville) specifically for dyslexic children. It seemed the decision was being made for us. We sold the restaurant and the brownstone and moved to Connecticut.

Lakeville gave both of us all the things we said we wanted. For me, it was an outdoor life with horses and dogs, good schools for the kids, and a sense of space around me: never again would I have to negotiate the manic traffic on Flatbush Avenue. For Robert, it was the racetrack at Lime Rock less than three miles from our house, a large garage to house his car collection, and two hours closer to Maine.

Life took on a veneer of calm. Robert was attending AA and making friends all over town. It was a life of leisure, but one filled with activity. In between shuttling the kids to and from school and afterschool activities, I was riding horses, walking dogs, and getting involved in the inevitable committees that seem to accompany grade school. I took a course to become an EMT and joined the Salisbury Volunteer Ambulance Squad.

I knew that Robert would soon find a new all-encompassing focus. He often circled through his various interests, and he started taking photographs again. We talked about his renewing his architect's license so he could practice in Connecticut and discussed the idea of buying properties that we would renovate and resell. I was unprepared for what he proposed as his next chapter.

It was a mild spring night. McCullough and Jack were doing their homework.

"Let's go for a drive," Robert said.

"Where?" I asked.

"I don't know. Does it matter? I just thought it would be fun."

"Okay, don't get tetchy. Let me tell the kids, and I'll be right out."

Robert chose the fire-hydrant yellow Fiat Dino. Just sitting in the car his mood improved.

"Where would *you* like to go?" he asked.

"Hmm, how about through Salisbury, up Route 41, toward Great Barrington?"

He revved the engine and drove in silence for a few minutes.

"I have an idea I want to run by you," he said, throwing a smile in my direction. "You know how I've done really well investing some of the kids' money in Apple? And you know that when I suggested to U.S. Trust that they include it in our portfolio, they said it was still too risky?" Apple had been around since the late '70s but it was only with the introduction of iPods and iTunes that it started to see a marked increase in its stock value.

"I think the bank's too conservative. The market is doing really well, and our portfolio is lagging. Apple is only the tip of the iceberg. The bank doesn't appreciate the value of tech stocks. Anyway, I've been thinking about this a lot and doing some research, and I think I could invest our money at least as well as U.S. Trust is doing, and probably a lot better."

He took my silence as an invitation to continue.

"You know there's a whole world out there of people who invest their own money. And there are online classes I can take, and support groups of people who share what they've learned. TD Ameritrade is practically mainstream. Of course, the bank might not like it, but they can't stop me, and besides, you know, we have to pay them a fee; they don't do it for free, and, honestly, I don't think they're doing a very good job."

Robert looked at me.

"Well?" he said.

I was silent because I was still grappling with the concept. He was clearly serious. To say the first thing that popped into my head and out of my mouth would be, "You must be out of your fucking mind." For once, I didn't react first and think later. I was trying to understand, without asking him just yet, what was behind this idea. Was this something he'd always wanted to do and just hadn't talked about? Unlikely. I knew he chafed at having to ask the bank for additional disbursements. We received a monthly allowance that was based on our expenses and available dividends. Robert often quoted the number-one rule of good investing: don't touch the principal. He also often broke that rule.

This was his grand plan? Robert would take total control of the money that he had inherited from his grandparents, his mother, and his aunt; the money that had been carefully managed for generations and had steadily increased over the decades; the money that Robert was spending on idle thoughts and honest endeavors both; the money that afforded Robert his life of cars and boats and summers in Maine; the money that sent his children to expensive schools and allowed us to move through life with ease and generosity; the money that landed in his lap by the grace of God or good luck—this money was what he wanted to take charge of and be responsible for?

"Well, I guess, I really am not sure what to say. I'm surprised, obviously. I know you've done well by the kids, but that's just one stock. It seems to me that U.S. Trust is actually doing just fine. Maybe they're missing some opportunities, but on the whole they do a good job, and the money is safe."

"The money will be safe. What are you saying? That I'm just going to spend it?"

Of course, that was exactly what I was afraid of. To say so wouldn't be productive. How do you talk with someone when you think the entire conversation shouldn't even be happening in the first place? There was not an iota of me that thought it was a good idea, or that Robert would make a success of it. He was convinced that just as he'd had a career as a photographer, architect, and chef, this was simply one more feather that he would add to his cap as a Renaissance man. The conversation soon devolved into open disagreement.

After days of arguing, berating, pleading, and accusing traded back and forth, I finally gave up and threw down a meaningless threat.

"I can't stop you, but if you blow it, then we're through. I will divorce you."

He didn't hesitate or hedge. "I'm not going to blow it. Why can't you trust me?"

I should have stopped him—though I'm not entirely sure I had the authority to. I've asked myself many times, Did I give in because I didn't think I had the right to tell him what to do with his money? If so, why after fifteen years of marriage did I still see it as his money and not ours? Did I give in because I was so sure he was going to fail, and if he did it would prove I was right? Well, that would be stupid and self-defeating—and probably closest to the truth.

Eighteen months later, in October 2008, the market melted down. It was, in fact, the beginning of a years-long global financial crisis. Alan Greenspan, chair of the Federal Reserve in the years prior to the debacle, testified before Congress that it was a "once-in-a-century credit tsunami." Robert consoled himself that he wasn't alone; greater minds than his hadn't seen it coming either. I wasn't consoled. I also was no longer in a position to follow through on my promise to end the marriage if he blew it. If we'd lived in a big house, this probably would have been the moment we started sleeping in separate bedrooms. We didn't. But now there was an invisible wall running down the middle of our bed.

I wrapped myself in a veneer of civility so I wouldn't say on a daily basis what I thought of him. Robert didn't think he should be punished for being caught up in a worldwide crisis. I thought he was too forgiving of his own failings, and I wasn't anywhere close to forgiving him. We were stalemated. Life would go on.

I took a part-time job at the local wine store. It was fun, and while the income hardly made a difference, I felt I was part of the solution rather than part of the problem. It was an easy job to get; I was overqualified, and I knew the owners. But soon enough, McCullough would be going off to college and Jack would be going to the Putney School for the tenth grade. My job as a full-time mom was coming to an end. It was time to think about a full-time, more long-term job, any of which would require a bachelor's degree.

I had dropped out of NYU in my senior year. I would be entering the workforce as a woman in her forties, without a college degree, with a ten-year gap in her résumé. My last career job had been as a writer/ producer in the marketing department of Lifetime Television. There was no TV industry in the northwest corner of Connecticut. I would need to start over.

It seemed to me the first step was to go back to college and get my degree. One night after dinner, I broached the subject with Robert. He had three degrees: a BA, and two MAs, in photography and architecture. I assumed he would be enthusiastic. His first response was, "I don't think we can afford it." Under the circumstances I could understand why he thought that and yet there was nothing Robert ever wanted to do that we couldn't afford.

I was still thinking about how to respond when he said, "I've been thinking about opening another restaurant." The restaurant in Park Slope had been exhausting, expensive, and led to a relapse of drinking. He was lucky to sell it. I couldn't believe he wanted to do that again.

"It will be different this time. Now I know what I'm doing. It will be easier, simpler, trattoria-style. And we already own all the china and glassware, all the stuff from Vaux that's stored in the garage."

In one breath he'd moved the conversation from what I wanted to what he wanted, with no possibility of doing both.

I'd been doing research on where I could finish my degree. I'd requested my transcript from NYU. It was a document of failure. Poor grades. Incompletes. A mishmash of studies that didn't add up to a major or even a minor: Spanish, French, modern dance, art history, film, and theater. It wouldn't be a matter of just taking a course or two to finish. I'd gone to NYU to study theater, but now if I was to pick a major, it would be literature and writing.

I looked for Continuing Ed programs around me. There weren't many in the area. I could go to UConn Extension in Torrington, but I would have to take quite a few mandatory subjects. And most of the classes were at night. It's a dreary drive to Torrington in the daylight. I couldn't see myself leaving the house around dinnertime when it was already dark to attend a class on statistics.

Columbia University offered a General Studies degree. That could work. Go down to the city for three days a week, stay with friends. Study on the train. I was imagining a life that didn't involve Robert, except for his holding down the fort at home. A role he had never yet played. And Robert wasn't interested in helping me figure it out.

I would bide my time. Greenings was for sale. Mentally and emotionally, I had one foot out of the marriage. I agreed to help him open his restaurant—on the condition that he could find investors. And I continued to look at online job boards and the Help Wanted section in our local paper, *The Lakeville Journal.* One day I saw they were looking for a copyeditor. I had a general sense of what a copyeditor did, though I looked up the definition just to be sure. I hastily reworked my résumé to focus on any writing I had done since my days at Lifetime and applied for the position.

The paper was in a large, nondescript two-story building at the end of a short road off the main street in Lakeville. It had housed the printing presses, but they were long gone as everything was computerized. My interview was with the editor, Cynthia, a tall, slender woman whose office door was open to the newsroom, a space filled with a mismatched assortment of desks and chairs that looked like they'd been acquired at a bankruptcy sale. If I were a set designer for a newsroom drama, it would be styled just like this, I thought.

Patrick, the most veteran reporter in the room, looked like the TV detective Columbo. He smoked a cigar and wore a trench coat. Bernie, the layout editor, was the oldest of the group. He was a history and nature buff prone to wearing well-worn L.L. Bean apparel, and he could tell you anything you wanted to know about the esoterica of everything. Daryl, the managing editor with a bird's nest of facial hair, had a Ren-fair fixation. Marsden, the editor of the separate Arts & Entertainment section, with an eerie resemblance to her rescue greyhounds, was a talented photographer. Janet, the publisher, whose office was upstairs, was the only one I found intimidating. Most of the staff had personality with a capital *P*, but Janet's serious demeanor kept the train on its track.

But it was Cynthia I wanted to work with. She was stylish but casual. Easy to talk to, endlessly curious. I instinctively felt we had a lot in common. She had a daughter Jack's age, and a quirky, difficult husband. She'd moved up from the city around the same time I did. Cynthia also had a background in media. She'd been at *Metropolitan Home* magazine when I was at Lifetime. We were both fascinated with obituaries, which was perfect, because helping the families and funeral directors craft a fitting tribute to the deceased was part of the copyeditor's job.

Three months after I was hired, Cynthia gave me my first writing assignment. Every June the Morris Dancers came through Salisbury. A troupe of eight or so men and women dressed in white pants and tops, with red sashes, and bells strapped to their legs, shaking tambourines, and waving white handkerchiefs, they would dance around the gingko tree in the space behind the bank that served as an unofficial town square. Every June, the paper would do a story with a picture or two. It was a hokey but local tradition. Over the years, Cynthia, Patrick, and even Bernie had exhausted their descriptive powers. Writing about the Morris Dancers was the rite of passage for a new reporter. I must have done a good enough job, as Cynthia then asked me if I wanted to cover the Halloween Haunted House tour at The Mount, Edith Wharton's home in the Berkshires. Of course I did! Would I write about the Millbrook Horse Trials and Fitch's Corner Horse Trials? No one at the paper knew anything about horse sports. It would be a huge favor. How about the fundraiser for the Hotchkiss Library in Sharon? I could interview one of the twenty best-selling authors who lived in the area, who would be there signing copies of their books. Absolutely I would.

Cynthia believed that her reporters did their best work when they were writing about things they knew well. Patrick had a regular fishing column. Bernie wrote often about W. E. B. Du Bois, who was born in nearby Great Barrington. Within the year every interest in my life found its way in some form into the pages of *The Lakeville Journal*.

Slowly it dawned on me that this job was the equivalent of going back to college. I might not be awarded a degree for it, but I had a new career, as a writer and journalist. And Robert had nothing to do with it.

THE BIRKIN OR ME

MARCH 2010

"There's a car I want to buy," Robert announced. We were driving to Aiken, South Carolina, to spend a week with the kids. It was their spring break. They'd agreed to meet us in Aiken where many of my friends from Millbrook spent the winter. We were about eight hours into the trip, waiting for a call from our lawyer in Maine. Raven's Point, the house on Greenings that Robert couldn't live without and now could no longer afford, had finally gone to contract. It was scheduled to close that day.

At about two in the afternoon, Robert's cell phone rang. The money had been wired into our account. Greenings was part of our past.

"I'm assuming we're going to do what we've always done and take a little money for ourselves. You know how I've always wanted a Caterham Super 7. Well, this car I have in mind is cheaper. It's a Birkin. There's a place in Texas—"

"Robert, no! This has to stop. If you want the Birkin, then sell the Alfa or the Lola. They're your *toys*. You can do what you want with them. I'm not saying you can't have it. I'm just saying you can't take the family's money to buy it."

"That's ridiculous. There's plenty of money. Why do you think you get to be in charge?"

"Because there isn't plenty of money. There won't be any more windfalls. This is it. This is our chance to get spending under control. The Greenings money is not up for grabs."

"I've been planning on getting this car. I've already ordered it. It will look bad if I drop out now."

"So sell one of your other cars."

"I'm not gonna do that!"

"Well, let me put it this way: if you buy the Birkin, we're done."

"Are you kidding me?" Robert slammed his hands on the steering wheel. "You're really going to play that card again?"

It's true. It was my default position, the stick I used to try and make him behave. I'd said it so many times, and not done it, of course he didn't believe me. I'd expected him to want to take some money for himself, but I'd held out hope that maybe this time would be different. That the debacle of 2008, just two years prior, would have taught him some amount of caution, that at the very least he would be embarrassed by his failure, and hesitant to ask. I had hoped for better from him. I was disappointed but I wasn't surprised. And he wasn't asking; he was claiming it as his right.

"Robert, I'm tired of being the policeman. I'm tired of this same old script, over and over. I should have divorced you when you insisted on taking all the money from U.S. Trust and investing it yourself. I'm mad at myself that I didn't. But I'm not doing this dance with you anymore. You blew it. So, yes, I'm in charge now."

"You can't keep blaming me for that! It wasn't my fault, Tara. The market collapsed on everyone. When are you going to let that go? You're such a bitch."

"That's it. I'm not going to talk about it anymore. You do what you want. You always do. And I'll do what I want. When we get back to Lakeville, I'm calling a lawyer."

With those words came the relief of resolution. I'd been in a holding pattern for two years. While I was waiting for Greenings to sell, I'd started building a life separate from Robert. My job at the paper, while only part-time, gave me a reason to stay in Lakeville during the summer, the best season for riding. There were events to compete in and volunteer for. I'd done my time on boats; I no longer felt obligated to go for Robert's sake. The sale of Greenings freed me. McCullough and Jack were old enough to go to Maine without me; they could go with Robert and stay with my sisters or friends.

We continued on to Aiken. Neither of us brought the subject up again. Pretending that everything was okay, for our children's sake, and for the harmony of the vacation, we went through the week finding relief and room to breathe. Decades of accumulated tensions seemed to dissolve. We visited with our friends, shopped and cooked meals together, went to a shooting range with our friend Woody, who remarked that I was an excellent shot and said, "Better be careful, Robert. You wouldn't want to make her mad." Robert and I looked at each other and laughed, sharing a private joke that Woody couldn't get.

I wondered if he'd called the outfit in Texas and canceled the order, or if he'd arranged to have the car shipped. I wondered if he would sell one of his other cars or if he was going to choose the Birkin over us. I was content to wait to find out.

I'd finally accepted that Robert was who he was and nothing I said or did was going to change him. It was I who changed. I was no longer investing energy in his outcomes. I helped out at the restaurant, but only if it was convenient for me. It wasn't our restaurant. It wasn't my dream. In removing myself from his equation I was freeing us both. Robert was never against me; he was just for himself. I still thought that selfish, given that we were married and meant to support each other, but my judgment about it was different. I gave myself permission to pursue my interests, to live my life first.

Our marriage, our relationship had become defined by a pattern that didn't serve me. And while it looked like it was serving Robert, in many ways it wasn't either. When we divorced, he had to change many things. He moved to a smaller space in town. A house that had been converted to a retail space, with an apartment on the second floor. He moved the restaurant into the ground floor. It was a building he'd always liked, and had considered when he first looked at locations for Café Giulia.

The fight we had in the car on the way to South Carolina was pretty much the last fight we had. We found a lawyer in Litchfield who mediated divorces. We met with her three or four times, hammering out the details. There wasn't much left to divide. Robert agreed to pay me a small amount of alimony for a couple of years, but I knew what his assets were, and I didn't expect him to support me long-term. I had learned I could take care of myself.

TWENTY-THREE DAYS TO LIVE

TUESDAY, JUNE 5, 2012

Tuesday was deadline day at *The Lakeville Journal*. The day the paper was put to bed. As copyeditor I read every story at least twice, looking for typos, broken continuity, missing photo credits, misspellings in headlines, style and format errors; no detail was too small. I even checked the number of spaces between words. It was exacting work, and I loved it. I like efficiency, precision, and order. It was the perfect job for a Type A control freak, which I didn't think I was, but Robert called me that. He refused to load the dishes in the dishwasher.

"What's the point?" he asked. "You're just going to restack them."

"Uh-huh, but if you put all the big plates together and the small plates together on the other side, then I wouldn't have to."

On Tuesday, June 5, I was having a hard time focusing on those little spaces between the words. I was waiting for the day to be over so I could go visit Robert. He wasn't feeling well, and I was worried about him. I'd seen him the night before and thought he looked awful—alarmingly thin. When had he lost so much weight? He carried himself erect but walked slowly, as though each step was causing him pain. Yet there he was in the kitchen of his restaurant. Café Giulia. He'd named it not after a woman, as one might assume, but after his car, an Alfa Romeo Giulia Super Ti, which he often parked on the lawn in front of the building.

He was wearing his black chef's jacket with his name embroidered on the upper left pocket, the clip of a meat thermometer peeking out, and a black chef's cap. I had come in after work, looking forward to having Robert cook for me, hoping that if it wasn't busy, he would sit with me for a few minutes, and we could catch up on things. He saw me come in and came toward me.

"What's wrong?" I asked, alarmed.

"I'm not sure. I'm waiting to find out. I went to see Dr. Parker today. I thought it was my ulcer kicking up, so I've been taking Nexium, but over the weekend the pain radiated around to my back."

Dr. Parker was concerned about Robert's weight loss and the pain. They'd done blood work, which showed elevated enzyme levels. The doctor immediately ordered a CAT scan. Robert was told he could expect test results the next day.

The restaurant was closed on Tuesdays, so I let myself in the kitchen door and climbed the stairs to his apartment. He was expecting me. He waved me inside. He was on the phone but finished the call as I came in and kissed him. Dr. Parker had already called with the results, a half-hour before. "It's not good news," Robert said.

Dr. Parker had asked him to come down to the office.

"You know it's bad when they say that."

Robert didn't want to get up and drive the twenty minutes to Parker's office, wondering all the way, Just how bad is it? He'd asked Parker to give him the news on the phone.

Robert looked at me. "It's liver cancer." He said it the way you might say, "It's bratwurst," in answer to "What's that?"

He was calm. In some ways, he'd been expecting this—or something like it—all his life. This current diagnosis could be the result of the radiation he'd had for a Wilms tumor, the kidney cancer he'd had as a four-year-old. The treatment used in 1955 could have killed him just as easily as the cancer itself. Maybe it was killing him now. The radiation, having lain dormant for fifty-five years, could be the cause of the tumors in his liver.

Then, too, Robert drank. Though he'd spent decades enjoying every kind of cocktail, wine, and cognac in excess, Robert had taken his last drink more than eight years before. But with the diagnosis of liver cancer, he also found out he had cirrhosis. So, was it the drinking or the radiation? Both? Did it matter?

For years I'd lived with the fear that something bad would happen to Robert. I had moments when I felt overwhelmed with grief at the thought of losing him, of being in the world without him. He'd had cancer, he drank, he smoked, he raced cars. I could work myself up imagining the dangers and the scenarios that would take him away from me. But he'd safely reached the age of sixty and was *fine*. Yet now, what I'd expected for years and then finally stopped worrying about was in fact happening. And it was like nothing I'd imagined.

We sat facing each other, Robert on the kilim sofa we'd picked out together, his feet propped up on the glass coffee table in front of it, me curled up on the black velvet chair he'd bought before we met. I looked around the room, identifying the landmarks of Robert's life by the objects that filled the bookshelves and decorated the walls. The teak signboard from his grandfather's boat, *Monaloa,* hung over the doorway, its letters outlined in gold paint. There was a large black-and-white photograph of the Borghese Gardens in Rome that we'd bought after our first trip to Italy. The art nouveau card table he'd carried twenty blocks from the store in SoHo because he didn't want to wait for it to be delivered. The two-foot-high bronze Shiva had been his mother's. Model cars of Ferraris and Alfas were scattered among shelves of books on classic cars and racing. The block of wood that he'd brought home from a gallery, and I'd asked, "You paid money for that?" When we'd divided up the art during our divorce, there was no debate over that piece.

The apartment was filled with things collected during our life together. After nearly twenty-two years of marriage, we'd gotten divorced twenty months earlier. We had agreed it was the end of our marriage but not our relationship. True to say that we were family. Entwined, still. We lived less than a mile away from each other. We co-owned the house we'd shared. Robert's cars were in the garage. His office down in the basement was intact.

I told him, "Whatever you need me to do, you know I will. If you need me to put the house on the market before next year, we can."

The terms of our divorce allowed me to live in the house until Jack, who was sixteen at the time of the divorce, went away to college, then it would have to be sold. Robert was anxious for me to sell it sooner; in fact, we'd met with a real estate agent just the month before to discuss it, but I'd backed off. Now it seemed like he might need his share of the money from the sale of the house. Cancer is expensive.

Years earlier, when I'd imagined the life of divorced parents—entangled because of shared custody, negotiated holidays, the introduction of a new significant other, possible stepchildren—these thoughts were enough to reinforce my willingness to make our marriage work. I couldn't see how, if Robert and I didn't get along when we supposedly loved each other, we were going to manage when we no longer had a stake in making each other happy. When we did finally decide to divorce, those fears no longer existed: the children were almost grown, and we weren't making each other happy anyway.

Now I imagined the rituals of grown-up divorced couples. Shared holidays—Robert still presiding over our table, but maybe his girlfriend, my boyfriend, would both be there as well. The blended family—Robert and me, our children still at its core. Robert would certainly remarry. I saw his new wife and me—would we be sitting in the same pew?—watching as Robert walked our daughter down the aisle at her wedding. He would be openly crying, overcome with emotion, sentimental as he was. He used to talk about that. Not the scenario with the new wife but that he fully expected to cry more than anyone else when McC got married. It was one of the things I first loved about him, his apparent easy access to his emotions.

He wasn't going to walk his daughter down the aisle.

We sat and talked for the next two hours.

"You know I broke up with Susan?"

"I heard. What happened?"

"She needed me to be there in a way I just couldn't." Susan was a woman Robert had met on eHarmony. She was an artist and lived in New Hampshire. They'd been seeing each other even before our divorce was final. Robert had told me a few weeks before he moved out that he was "going to hit the ground running."

"You may not be interested in sex, but I am, and I'm not waiting."

I wasn't shocked by what he said, but I was surprised that he could still hurt me. It was so typical. Patience wasn't one of Robert's virtues, and he had admittedly a limited interest in self-reflection. It wasn't lost on me that it was a repeat of his behavior when he'd separated from his first wife. The night of the day Colby had moved out, Robert and I went out to dinner, and he came home with me.

I knew that Susan had been sick. I wondered if cancer was one of the things that had brought them together. She had a history of breast cancer. When they started dating, it was in remission. But while they'd been together, she had a series of setbacks. The latest had something to do with her heart.

Robert said, "This won't surprise you, but she wants more than I give her. You know how selfish I am." He said this with a wry smile. "Also, I don't want to be known as the cancer couple."

I *was* surprised, actually. Robert always came first in our marriage, but he and Susan had seemed happy together. She lived two and a half hours away, so there was some traveling involved, but she came to Lakeville a lot. She was independent. She had her own home, life, career. I'd assumed that she was less demanding than I and that Robert was more giving in return. Driving by the restaurant one weekend afternoon, I saw the two of them in the window, putting up new curtains.

"Hah, more power to you, Robert," I thought. That used to be me. It was a job I was happy to relinquish. I'd put my time in helping Robert fulfill his dreams, believing that I was indispensable. It was a role I'd created for myself. I would be heroic in what I would contribute. I would never say no when asked to help. Seeing Susan and Robert, it occurred to me that I was never indispensable. There would always be someone else to help put up curtains. And I wanted Robert to have someone to help him. He didn't like to be alone. He needed to have a playmate. I wanted him to be a better partner to Susan than he'd been to me, so that she'd stick around. I thought, maybe it's easier to be the person you want to be, with someone new. Carrying decades of baggage and bad behavior around weighs you down. It's hard to escape the roles we cast ourselves, and each other, in. Long after we tired of the script, we found ourselves repeating the same lines, replaying the same scenes.

Robert said, "I hear you and Donald broke up." I had also moved on after our divorce. Donald was considerably older than I, and a confirmed bachelor. It was an unsatisfying relationship.

"Yeah, we did."

"That's good." Robert smiled.

We talked about what a diagnosis of liver cancer might mean. We knew it was a death sentence, but we didn't know how soon. We talked about what he might do, both for treatment and in the time he had left. His friend Pete, who had hepatitis, had had five liver transplants. Surely that was a possibility for Robert as well. Parker had scheduled another CAT scan and an MRI, both for the next day. He wanted to find out if the cancer had metastasized from another location, which would be very bad, or had started in the liver, which was quite bad enough.

"What difference does it make?"

"They have to know what kind of cancer it is to know how to treat it," he told me. Also, they would do a biopsy. Those results could take four or five days.

"That's crazy," I said. "I thought the idea was to start treatment as soon as possible. I've heard of people getting a diagnosis and starting treatment the next day. I think we should talk to Parker again."

"Tara, settle down. You're going to have to let me handle this my way. This is not your fight."

The only way I knew how to deal with news like this was to *do* something. Problems were to be solved. If something was wrong, it needed to be fixed. If it was broken, it needed to be mended. This was how I operated. Robert was more inclined to sit back and let things run their course. He had always lived as though he might die tomorrow. He had a line he invoked every time we had a disagreement about something he wanted to do or buy. If I had any resistance, he would say, "I don't know how long I have to live. Now is the time for me to do this."

"That's selfish," I would say. "None of us knows how long we have to live."

Sitting with Robert, knowing that his end was in sight, I realized he may have been right. When I'd been in the midst of it, in competition for his time, attention, and money, I had begrudged him every selfish thought. I fought against that reasoning. "If you only have a short time to live, this is what you would choose? Go race a car instead of spending time with your family? If you only have a short time to live, what does it matter if you own that Ferrari or this Alfa? Are these the things that are most important to you?"

In fights like those, he accused me of being a *puritanical moralist.* I shot back that he was "a self-indulgent alcoholic, the kind that gives trust funds a bad name." And yet he had lived his life the way he wanted and hadn't missed much.

We talked about the kids and how and when we'd tell them. Jack was graduating from the Putney School in five days. McCullough was home from college, but she and her boyfriend were going back and forth to New York City a lot. We wanted to tell them when we were all together. We didn't want to tell McCullough without telling Jack, and we didn't want to tell him on the phone.

We talked about how he'd manage the restaurant. He had a good staff and a sous-chef he trusted, but we both knew from experience that restaurants don't run themselves. And the truth was, people came to the restaurant to see *him*. He talked about maybe finding someone to buy it. But I suspected it wouldn't take much for him to shut it down. Robert wasn't the guy who dutifully clocked into the same job for decades. There had been many times I judged him to be morally deficient for his lack of commitment, but now I was sympathetic. The restaurant was a lot of work. Who would want to cook every night and fight cancer at the same time?

What we didn't talk about was the fact that I was leaving for Bennington in ten days. A few months after our divorce, I was helping Jack with his college applications. We were looking at the Bennington College website, and I saw a page that said, "Read 100 Books, Write One." Oh my god, who wouldn't want to do that? I thought. Well, Jack, for one. He didn't apply to Bennington. But I did.

It was a master's program, and I didn't have a bachelor's degree. Years before, a friend of mine who'd dropped out of Columbia was admitted to Syracuse University's master's program because of his work history. They called it life credits. This was the solution I hadn't seen three years before when I first raised the subject of returning to school to Robert; when I didn't want to take a slew of required courses anyway, and all I really wanted to do was read books and discuss them. And write. On the strength of my work for *The Lakeville Journal,* Bennington agreed to give me life credits and accepted my application.

Robert had said, "We can't afford it." After our divorce, it was even more of a financial reach. Except now I didn't need his agreement to spend money. He'd given me a sizeable diamond ring for our tenth wedding anniversary. I sold it to pay for the tuition. It was the perfect trade-off.

When Robert said, "It's cancer," my first thoughts were concern for him, and our children, but just behind that flitted this: Are you kidding me? I'm finally free of you, about to go back to school, and you're going to get sick and die, at exactly the same time? It seemed that every time I put myself first, Robert found a way to demand it back. The timing struck me as hugely ironic.

Robert told me that he'd been emailing with Colby, his first wife. He had stayed in touch with her over the years. Once when our children were young, she'd come to dinner in Brooklyn, and every Christmas she sent our family a card. She'd remarried sometime in the past five years. Robert and Colby didn't have children, and though on some level it probably pained her, she seemed happy to see him reflected in our children. She was going to visit sometime in the next few weeks, Robert told me. She wanted to come and eat at the restaurant.

But first he was going to go to Maine with the kids.

"Maybe you could get off work and come up for some of the time? It would be nice for all of us to be together."

As I left, I said, "Come home whenever you want, whenever you're ready."

"Thanks," he said, "but there's no rush."

FULL CIRCLE

MONDAY, JUNE 25, 2012

I returned from Bennington on Sunday. I'd gone ahead despite his diagnosis. The doctors said he might have two years. We would try to live life as normally as possible. He would keep the restaurant going and then take the kids to Maine for a couple of weeks. We'd talked about McCullough and what might happen with her college plans. Robert didn't want her to drop out or take a leave of absence. He wanted life to go on as normal, as planned. Maybe toward the end, he said, she might take a semester off. Jack was closer by. He was about to graduate from high school. He could take a year off, a gap year, like McCullough had done. He would probably be happy about that.

Robert never suggested that I shouldn't go on with my Bennington plans, but the day I was to leave he had a biopsy scheduled and asked if I could take him to the hospital, wait, and drive him home. "Sure," I said. I saw then that if I had to make a choice, if things got really dire, I would choose Robert over Bennington. It would always be there. He wouldn't.

Before I left, Robert and I sat down with our children to tell them about his diagnosis. We asked them to come and sit with us in the living room. "We have something to tell you," I said by way of explanation. I thought about McCullough's boyfriend, Luke, and how he was being drawn unwittingly into an intimate family drama. I thought, it will say a lot about him to see how he helps McCullough deal with this news. Hesitancy and fear registered on their faces. It seemed to occur to Robert and me simultaneously that the last time we had a conference like this was when we told them we were getting a divorce.

He made a bad joke. "Your mom and I are getting back together."

No one laughed.

"Robert!" I scolded him.

He then told them that he'd been diagnosed with liver cancer. They asked what that meant.

"Well, it's not good," he acknowledged. He said that he was going to fight it, that there were treatments. He might be able to get a liver transplant, like his friend Pete. "It's too early to say."

"We don't know what's going to happen, but we'll take it one day at a time."

McCullough leaned forward, intently absorbing her father. Jack sat quietly, his thoughts not registering on his face.

"Sarah and John are going to come for a visit while Mom's at Bennington."

My sister's husband, John, was one of Robert's closest friends. Sarah's a trust officer and a lawyer and would help Robert get his papers organized.

"We can help, too," McCullough said.

Robert stood and we all got up. Jack went over and hugged his dad, and then McCullough did too. They stood the three of them with their arms around each other for a moment, before moving away.

I'd been away for ten days. Ten days during which Robert and I had only spoken on the phone. I called him every morning, not too early, because I didn't want to wake him, and I called him at the end of the night, when I thought that he would be back upstairs in his apartment above the restaurant—the customers gone, the stainless-steel containers of food covered tightly in cling wrap and refrigerated, his knives carefully cleaned, dried, and stored in his knife roll, the night's receipts tallied, another shift over.

Three days before I returned, Robert went to New York to see a holistic oncologist. Brian went with him. He left the appointment with $500 worth of supplements and vitamins but not much hope. A friend had driven him into the city, but he took the train back and was exhausted by the time he got home.

Then the next day he went to Lime Rock Park to hang out with his racing friends. I'd called him during a break between lectures and could hear the sounds of the racetrack in the background. His voice was strong. He sounded energetic. He sounded like the Robert I knew.

As I left campus the next day, I called him again. I wanted to make plans for that evening. He was having brunch with friends.

"Do you want to come up to the house for dinner tonight? Or should the kids and I come down to the restaurant? What would you like to do?"

He didn't have a preference. Making decisions seemed too difficult. Anything was okay.

"Then come up to the house. I'll make something simple. It'll be more relaxed."

When Robert arrived, I was shocked by his appearance. When I met him all those decades ago, he had a slightly receding hairline but abundant wavy silver hair. Then a few years ago, Robert started cutting his hair very short. With his hair that length, he already looked like someone who was either going through chemo or recovering from it. Now everything about him said *Cancer*. He was smaller, frailer, weaker. But what alarmed me was his lack of focus.

We sat at the kitchen table, a family together again. We didn't talk about his health. We made plans for the coming week. McCullough and Luke were going to the city for a few days; they would return on Wednesday. I was expected back at the *Lakeville Journal*. Jack was going to try and see some friends. He'd be around if Robert needed help at the restaurant. I looked at Robert. His eyes were closed. He'd fallen asleep. I gently took the fork out of his hand. After dinner, he went downstairs to the TV room to hang out with the kids. I took the dogs for a walk, telling him before I left, "When you're ready to

go, I think I should drive you back to the restaurant. You're very tired."
He didn't argue.

He still had to supervise closing up and pay out the weekly tips. We were sitting in his apartment above the restaurant waiting for the last customers to leave when I asked him, "Isn't it time for you to take your Nexavar?" It was the only drug they'd prescribed to fight the tumors. It was like chemo in a pill, but at best it would only slow the growth.

Robert had told me he was taking it at 10 p.m. every night. I'd been with him for hours and I hadn't seen him take it. "No, no," he said, "I took it already."

"Really? Because I thought you were taking it at 10, and it's just 10 now."

"No, I did," he insisted. "Look, I always write it down. It's in that book."

The book was the black-and-white composition book I'd brought with us to the first doctor's visit after his diagnosis. I knew how difficult it was to remember everything a doctor said and encouraged Robert to always have someone go with him to his appointments.

"Have them takes notes in this book," I'd told him.

I took it and paged through. Our friend Licia had gone on one appointment. There were the notes Brian had taken during the consultation with Dr. Gaynor. And in Robert's own handwriting, the log detailing the time and date he took the Nexavar. The last entry was two days before.

Robert grimaced and wailed, "Nooo."

"It's okay. It's okay." There's a way for us to figure it out, I told him.

"Where's the medicine? Look, it's in tablets. Let's just count them."

He'd only started taking them Wednesday; now it was Sunday. I emptied the bottle on the table in front of him, counting out the pills. He had taken them the past few days, but Sunday's pill was still in the bottle. I got him a glass of water to take the pill and updated the entries in the book.

"Do you want to come back to the house with me?"

"No. I'm going to watch a little TV, then go to bed."

"Okay, I'm going to go. Call me tomorrow, all right?" I kissed him and left.

The next morning Sheila, a friend of Robert's and mine, called me at the paper. She'd gone to see him, to help him sort out his already mounting medical bills.

"Tara, something's wrong. Robert seems really confused."

"I noticed that last night," I told her. "He was talking with us at dinner, and midsentence he started talking about something else entirely. I'll call Dr. Kruger."

I asked Sheila if she would stay with him until I could get there. Two hours later we were in the oncologist's office. Dr. Kruger examined him as I watched. He seemed surprised at how visible the tumor was. He palpated it gently.

"Is there pain?" he asked.

"Yes."

He prescribed more Vicodin, oxycodone. He wanted another blood test done. He listened to the story about the medication and the descriptions of losing lucidity and gently told Robert that he shouldn't be living alone. "You should be with your family now," he told Robert. "It's not safe for you to drive."

Hearing that, Robert clenched his fist and moaned. But he let me take his arm as we walked to the car. I drove to the hospital and waited while he got his blood drawn. When I'd accompanied him to the hospital for the biopsy, before I left, he'd been in charge, handling the paperwork and admission procedure himself. Now I felt like I was leading a child by the hand. Robert, who never hesitated to assert himself with me, to push back against any direction I might give, seemed happy to follow along, leaning on my arm. It was cozy and nice, even if the reason for it was awful.

We drove to the pharmacy in Salisbury, walking in side by side, and left the prescriptions to be filled. Robert seldom went anywhere in town without running into friends. There were his morning coffee friends, customers from his restaurant, anyone who had ever sat in an AA meeting with him, friends from the racetrack, the guys he played bridge or tennis with. We encountered Beth on the sidewalk. She and her husband, Jack, were two of Robert's closest friends. When Robert and I were still married, the four of us often had dinner together. "I'm so glad you're back," she said to me. "I'm so glad he's with you." She hugged him hard, said she would come see him tomorrow.

We drove to his apartment to collect a few things. I gathered the medicines from his bureau top and bedside table. There weren't many. From the beginning the doctors had said his cancer was generally untreatable. Mostly, he was taking drugs to treat the pain, to help him sleep, and to treat symptoms like indigestion. These drugs were for minor health problems, not life-threatening ones.

"What else do you want to take now? Some T-shirts, socks, underwear?" I asked.

"I don't need to bring a lot. I'll be coming back later," he said.

I didn't think he would, but I didn't say so.

I drove the short distance to the house. The house we had lived in together. Jack was home. He took his dad's arm and helped him inside. Robert wanted to lie down.

"Where?" Jack asked me.

"In my room."

"I can stay with Dad tonight, if you want," Jack said. I could see his concern for Robert etched on his face. I tried to reassure him. Jack also was being considerate. His parents were divorced. Divorced people didn't share the same bed.

"No. It'll be fine, honey. Daddy and I can sleep in the same bed."

For twenty-two years Robert and I had shared a bed, and even though we hadn't shared that bed in nineteen months, it was trivial to think it mattered now. Robert needed to be looked after and that was something I knew how to do. I cleared my books and photos from what had been his bedside table and set out a water glass and his medicine.

AN AA MEETING

TUESDAY, JUNE 26, 2012

After Dr. Kruger told him it wasn't safe for him to be alone and he should be with his family, Robert came home, back to the house that had been ours but was now mine. The next morning he woke up abruptly and as he struggled out of our bed, he said, "I want to go to the meeting." He was referring to the 7 a.m. Alcoholics Anonymous meeting at St. Mary's Church. It was just a mile down the road.

"Okay," I said. "Give me a second. I'll get dressed and drive you."

Robert pulled on a pair of ripped and stained khakis and slid his bare feet into his beat-up boat shoes, the same uniform he'd been wearing when I met him two decades ago. Having him back in the house was as familiar to me as the clothes he was wearing. And yet it wasn't the same as before, not at all. Robert had changed since we divorced; he seemed happier, more content. He was nicer to me. He spent more time with his friends; he actually called people and issued invitations, proposed meeting for coffee or lunch. This wasn't the

Robert I lived with for years; he'd let people come to him; he seldom
made the phone call. Those duties had fallen to me. Since the diagnosis
he was reaching out a lot. He wasn't shy about telling people he was
sick. "I don't need to broadcast it," he told me, "but I'm not going to
hide it either."

Many of his regular customers at the restaurant had become new
friends and they more than others were aware of the physical change
in Robert. If they asked how he was in more than a casual way, he'd
tell them. Not everything, not the details, but that he had cancer and
was getting treatment.

The 7 a.m. meeting at St. Mary's was one that Robert and his
friend Randy had started about six years before. It was important to
him that he begin his day with a meeting, followed by coffee hour at
the Roast with his friends. This was his morning ritual. As much a part
of his life as cocktail hour used to be. Every AA meeting has its own
personality formed by the age, attitudes, and addictions of its members.
But meetings are not just for alcoholics, they're for addicts; it doesn't
matter what the drug of choice is. Robert preferred the meetings that
were mostly alcoholics. He didn't relate to twenty-year-old kids doing
meth or prescription drugs.

His recent commitment to the program had been strong; he
often opened the meetings, he served as a sponsor, he socialized with
people he met in the rooms, friends who'd become my friends too. I
kept my distance from the meetings. I never asked if or when he was
going. I never asked, "How was the meeting today?"

But spending time with Robert and his friends from the rooms let me be part of an increasingly significant part of his life. These people were in recovery. They had a lot to offer Robert, and me. Some were couples who were both in the program. Some were couples, one in recovery but one who still drank. Seeing how others coped, communicated, and got along with each other helped me keep perspective that the whole process was based on Progress Not Perfection. I loved the AA reminders. They were simple but elementally truthful: One Day at a Time, Keep It Simple, or Keep It Simple, Stupid—a little humility being a good thing.

I'd been in this room once before when Robert invited me to an anniversary meeting. It had been precipitated by the now-familiar stages of Robert's alcoholism: denial (he was drinking but wouldn't admit it); anger (he didn't like getting caught out); bargaining (rehab or else); acceptance (he went, but with resentment). I was surprised and happy when he invited me to celebrate his third year of sobriety. At the meeting, the room was packed. Robert wasn't the only person celebrating a milestone and I wasn't the only guest.

He stood up to share. He introduced himself and gave a brief account of his history and what the anniversary meant to him. Then he said, "I want to publicly acknowledge my lovely wife, Tara, without whom I would not be here today. She has been my biggest supporter, and I want her to know how much I appreciate her and love her."

My hands clenched the folding chair, and I sat rigid, seething. I could see heads nodding in agreement, smiles of affection for Robert and his sweet honesty, even heard a smattering of applause, as he accrued to himself the credit for recognizing in public what he would never tell me in private. It's not that I didn't want to hear those words. It's that I wanted him to tell *me*—not the room. Why did he need an audience to make such a declaration? Was this more role-playing? Acting the part of the devoted husband, which even at his best he never pretended to be. He'd never expressed that sentiment before. But I also knew that over the past three years, beyond insisting that he go back to rehab and go to meetings, I didn't think I had been particularly supportive, unless leaving him alone to figure it out by himself was support.

Now at a distance far removed from that day, I can say I would rather have heard it in the meeting than not at all.

I pulled into the parking spot close to the church entrance, the one reserved for the handicapped and elderly parishioners. I came around to open the car door and held his arm as we walked into the basement room. The meeting was already in progress, about fifteen people sitting in chairs arranged in a *U* shape. I saw Robert's friend Mike and waved. I also saw the mother of one of my children's friends and looked away. I felt like I'd outed her. Anonymity is the guiding principle in AA. The meetings are not for spectators. I was there for Robert. He was sick. It was a special circumstance in my mind. I guess I could have walked him to the door and come back at the end. I knew he wouldn't be without friends inside. But I didn't want to leave him.

We took seats against the wall, outside the circle. After a while, Robert cleared his throat to speak. "Hi, I'm Robert and I'm an alcoholic. I don't know how many of you know, but I have liver cancer." He talked about the unlikelihood of successful treatment, and he talked about acceptance. "I don't have any regrets," he said. "When I was in the shower the other day, I thought, why me? And then I thought, why not me?"

This was the most I'd heard Robert speak of his illness other than in practical, medical terms. I wondered if there was something about the rooms, or maybe just this room, that made Robert feel he could open up and say anything. Maybe when he talked about acceptance he meant the acceptance of his friends in the room, or even more, his acceptance of himself, of what was happening to him, of how far he had come, acceptance that his end was in sight and that he wasn't going to fight it. Afterward, many of his friends came up to us. They hugged him and said they would check in on him later. One woman said to me, "Welcome. It's nice to see you here."

We left and went to get coffee. There was a time it was a ritual we shared, until I started to get antsy and annoyed by the pace of it. The coffeehouse was small, with only a few tables, maybe sixteen seats in all. You could talk to anyone in the room without raising your voice. I got impatient with the circular, repetitive conversations. I felt like a spectator to Robert's friendships. I felt like I was there as proof that he had a life outside the Roast. But he never seemed to want to talk to me, even when we got there early and the regulars hadn't yet arrived.

It had been a few years since I'd joined Robert at coffee, and after we divorced, I considered it his space. Now it felt good to walk in there with him. To see familiar faces, hear the usual greetings, to sense that there in the Roast nothing ever changed. Not divorce, not death. Not the repetitive chat. It was a bubble I was happy to join Robert in, and to stay as long as he wanted. Robert had the day off from the restaurant. If there were deliveries, Dominic could check them in.

Late that afternoon, he was reclining on the couch in the living room when I called Dr. Kruger to get the results of the blood test and ask the question we hadn't asked when we were in his office—the question Robert didn't want to ask.

"How long does he have to live?"

"The blood work showed his liver and kidneys are shutting down," Dr. Kruger said. "He might have only two or three weeks more. It's time to call hospice."

"You have to be the one to tell him," I told the doctor. "It shouldn't be me."

I handed the phone to Robert and shortly after that he hung up. I sat next to him and took his hands in mine.

"What do you want to do?" I asked him. "Do you want to spend your last days traveling to the city, going to see more doctors?"

"Not really," he said and smiled. "But I don't mind if you do."

That was the last we spoke of his dying.

McCullough was in the city until Wednesday. After seeing Dr. Kruger on Monday, we'd discussed calling her and suggesting she return a day early. But we didn't want to alarm her. We didn't want McCullough or Jack to feel anxious. There was time, we thought, for us all to be together.

Now I said, "We should call McCullough."

"She's coming back tomorrow."

"I know, but she should know what's going on. Maybe she can come on an earlier train."

By the time I spoke to her it was nearly 7:30 p.m. We decided it didn't make sense for her to take the train then. She and Luke would return in the morning. I don't remember what we did that night. I'm sure I made dinner and then Jack, Robert, and I went downstairs to eat in front of the TV. I don't remember what we talked about. All the conversation about his health was technical, specific, practical. What next? What are the options? How are you feeling? Do you need me to get you anything? Often Robert seemed mildly annoyed by my attention. What were we going to say to each other in these last weeks that we had not said to each other in the more than twenty years we spent together?

"Why not me?" Robert had said in the meeting that morning. After years of demanding special treatment, of needing to stand out from the crowd, the Robert whose high school yearbook noted, "Robert Willis—Walks Like He Is"—that Robert seemed content to sit in front of the TV and watch an episode of *Law and Order*. No complaint, just acceptance.

ADRIFT

THURSDAY, JUNE 28, 2012

At 7 a.m., I'm in the kitchen making a cup of tea. I have Robert's cell phone with me. I call Susan in New Hampshire.

"Hi. It's Tara. Robert's here at home with me. I think it's near the end. If you want to see him, I think you should come today." She's crying and says she will find a friend to drive her. She'll arrive in a few hours.

I also expect Colby to arrive sometime in the morning. Recently remarried, she's driving down from upstate New York with her husband. Robert and Colby had recently reconnected by email. The visit had been arranged a few weeks before.

There are a few other people to call. Robert's sister Barbara is expecting to come on the weekend. Now I phone her: she should come immediately. I haven't even had a chance to tell our friend Wendy, who's living in London, that Robert is sick. Wendy is McCullough's godmother. Robert and I are her younger daughter Celeste's godparents. Robert and Wendy have always been especially close, having a shared history of summers in Maine, and both having opened restaurants. Now I'm calling to tell her he's dying. I've barely finished explaining the sequence of events, when Wendy says, "I'm on my way. I'll be there as soon as I can book a flight."

There's an email from Brendan: should he bring Robert a latté? I tell Brendan, no, we're set on the coffee front. My sister Ursula and her girlfriend, Kathy, are going to give him a bath and shave. Come by after 9:30.

Overnight, Robert has developed pneumonia. He's struggling to breathe. Kathy calls hospice: they will send a drug to ease his breathing. Ursula ups the dose of liquid morphine.

At midday, Jack's in the kitchen baking cookies. McCullough's in the bedroom sitting next to her father holding his hand. Tomas, who shared Robert's passion for racing Alfas and sold him the car that Robert named the restaurant after, sits at the kitchen table talking with some of Robert's other racing buddies. Haywood, who'd witnessed three decades of Robert's life, wanders through the house looking bereft. The driveway and yard are filled with cars. The front door is open. The dogs are unusually quiet in the mudroom.

I give up my place at Robert's side as the house fills with people come to say goodbye. A line forms outside my bedroom door, snaking through the dining room and into the kitchen. A steady stream of friends who want just one more minute of time with him. Evidence of how much people care. There are friends from the program, from the track, from the restaurant, from the neighborhood. There are some faces I recognize but cannot name.

It feels like a wake, but there will be no actual wake: Robert wasn't Catholic. There won't even be a funeral. We will have a memorial service in Salisbury a week later, at which his Alfa will be parked outside the Congregational Church. Two weeks after that we will scatter his ashes in the waters off Greenings Island.

Ursula explains to each new visitor what's happening to Robert, how his body is shutting down. "Hearing is the last sense to go," she says. "Robert can hear you. He may not be able to acknowledge you, but he can hear you. Tell him who you are and talk to him." I don't know if it is in fact true. But I've heard it said, and I want it to be.

When Susan arrives, I walk her down the hall past others who are waiting. I clear the room, leaving them alone together. Afterward, Susan and I sit together on the couch in the living room. I sympathize with her. I had twenty-five years with Robert. I had the luxury of time, and emotion. We had children together. Susan is bereft in a way I am not. She's mourning not just the loss of Robert, but the loss of possibility.

When Colby comes, she too will spend time alone with Robert and then seek out McCullough and Jack. A few months later she sends them a package: a photo album for each of them with photos from when Robert was a child.

Through it all, Robert lies in the bed, breathing softly. It seems like he's drifting. As though he's slipped his mooring and floats untethered, but the tide and currents of his gathered family and friends are keeping him close.

Over the course of the day, we see his body change. It's imperceptible at first, but in contrast to the morning, he looks less than. He's shrinking. It's finally clear to me that he will die soon.

We keep vigil. Knowing that he's dying, but not knowing when it will happen. It feels as if it's taking forever, and yet every time I leave the room, I worry that he will take his last breath while I'm away. His breathing slows, his face hollows.

Ursula suggests that anyone who wants to be with Robert at the end might want to come into the room. "Soon," she says. She's come outside to find me. She stops to talk with Jack, who's sitting on the lawn just outside the front door, sewing together some kind of camouflage tent. His way of dealing with this is to keep busy. She tells him that if he wants to be with his dad, he should come in. Jack thanks her but doesn't get up right away. I can't read his expression, but I suspect he can't bear to see his father die. I don't want to force him, but I know it's important for him to be there. I hold out my hand, and he slowly gets up and follows me in.

Around 4 p.m. the only cars left in the driveway are those of my family. As rapidly as people had flocked to the house, they also withdrew. We are alone with Robert.

Late in the afternoon, when he stops breathing, there are thirteen people surrounding him. It is absolutely still. So quiet, and yet we aren't sure which is his last breath. McCullough, Jack, and I sit side by side, next to him. I stroke his face. McCullough, in tears, and Jack, with his arm around his sister, each hold one of his hands. Haywood sits at the foot of the bed, head bowed, resting his hands on Robert's feet. John and Sarah, with her arm around their son, Max, Therese, my brothers, Brian and Justin, my sisters Maura and Ursula, with Kathy encircle the bed where Robert lies. No one speaks.

I think of how lucky Robert has been in life, and now in death. We didn't plan these last twenty-four hours. We all just came together to be with him, and while we were there, he died. Like so many events in Robert's and my life, it seemed to just happen. I think of how lucky we all are to be together, there in the room, with him.

Barbara doesn't arrive in time to see him alive. She calls. She's two hours away on the Mass Pike. I imagine what her drive's been like. If I didn't want to leave the room for even a few minutes, she must have felt like she was on the clock—a countdown to death. When I telephone Brian Kenny, the funeral home director whom I know well from editing the obits at the *Lakeville Journal,* I ask if he can come for Robert tonight but wait until after Barbara's seen him. No problem, he assures me.

I sit in the room with Robert, feeling that he shouldn't be left alone. I'm on my bed, the door to the room is partly open. No one joins me. As dusk comes, I switch on the bedside lamp so I can read while I wait.

EXCAVATION

Three years after Robert died, I decided to sell the house we'd shared and move twenty miles away to be closer to where most of my friends lived. It was time to shed some of the past. The symbolic weight of objects both meaningful and insignificant, but mostly not mine, needed to go. I was ready to start a new life for myself defined by neither Robert's presence nor his absence. The contents of the house and the outbuildings were a library of Robert's fluctuating and fading passions. Seventy-five boxes of books on architecture, design, photography, sailing, finance, Italian and French language, and cooking were carted off to nearby public libraries, most likely to end up in their annual book sales.

I alerted Robert's car buddies to the trove of tools, car parts, widgets, and gadgets that might interest them. I unpacked dozens of boxes that were stored from our move out of Maine only to put most of the things in the for-sale pile. I could have opened my own restaurant with the accumulated items left over from Vaux, his first restaurant

in Brooklyn, and then much of the contents of Café Giulia, which
remained open even on the day of his death, until I recognized the
insanity of that and pulled the plug two days later. I was sad to see the
heavy iron sauté pans, blackened and still a little greasy. I remembered
how enthralled Robert was with pollo al mattone, chicken-under-a-
brick, and how it became his signature dish. Even at the time I was
struck by how something so genuinely simple could speak to Robert.
I suspected that in his heart he saw himself as an Italian cook in
his trattoria, just cooking for his amici. I put aside three pans: for
McCullough, Jack, and myself.

I knew even as I was unloading this lifetime of things that there
might come a time when I would look for the green ceramic teapot or
some other memento from Greenings, forgetting that I had purged
them in this move. Nearly every item went through the same process—
memories unpacked and relived. The same evaluation applied. Stay?
Go? Don't know? Whatever I kept was destined for long-term storage,
because my plan was to move to a furnished rental. I didn't know where
or when I was going to have my own house again.

The things Robert held on to now seem like talismans of a vanishing
life. Back issues of Wooden Boat Magazine and boat models in glass
cases. He saved everything. Things from his grandparents' lives and
many more inherited from his mother; of course, he was a collector,
too. A few walking sticks from Gramps became the start of a new
collection, one I contributed to when I found, in an antique store in
Paris, a stick made from the vertebrae of a fish. The knob was a sailor's

monkey-fist knot of carved ebony. Now it's in a box with the others. In storage. Waiting for the day when either of our kids say, "Hey, whatever happened to Dad's cane collection?"

Moving meant I had to go through everything and consider if it should be kept for them. Neither had households or a place to store their father's memories and mementos. Which of his things would trigger their good memories of him? McCullough had gravitated to his cameras and selected some of his books on photography. Jack wanted little. It seemed he didn't want to think about it. So, I tried to put myself in their place, in their future, when maybe they would be more settled in their lives and ready to be attached to things. When maybe the pain of losing their father was not so acute and objects that were representative of him could be a source of comfort instead of a painful reminder of what they were missing.

As it turned out, Jack wanted the red Olympia espresso machine, the one I didn't remember he told me he wanted. The one I sold to my sister. Only I thought I gave it to her, and when I asked for it back, was reminded it wasn't that simple. A realization these many years later that objects can have intense emotional symbolism. So much for me being the keeper of their father's legacy.

Don't most of us accumulate and hold on to things? Things we don't need now but might need in the future. Things that remind us of who we were and maybe who we could have been, if we still used, liked, played, or mastered them. Things with their own language.

"You're going below, not downstairs," Robert told me when we were cruising on the chartered sailboat. "Winch the line! The sail is luffing." Winch? Luff? I'd probably heard those terms when I was at sailing camp, but I had to relearn them. Winch means pull it tight, and there's a little gizmo (the winch) on the rub rail that the line runs through that helps the sailor pull the rope. Luffing means flapping, and a flapping sail slows the boat. And the invaluable: "Ready about, hard-a-lee," which means we're changing directions, get ready to duck so you don't get knocked overboard by the boom as it swings by. The boom is that very heavy, long piece of wood that holds one side of the mainsail and could be the death of you. Maybe the language is the part I'll always keep with me.

Objects are easy enough to sell or give away, but papers and memorabilia are the talismans I hold on to. And yet there are so many boxes, I know I will have to be ruthless as I go through them. The compulsion to save every milestone of our children's development is evident in the mass of files organized by school and grade; the boxes of loose photos that never made it into a frame or a photo album but still evoke a memory worth savoring as I put them back and mark the box for storage. These are my collections. I know what's in each box by a peek inside, and I will deal with them another time.

I come across a stack of cards from Robert to me in their envelopes. Monday, Tuesday, Wednesday—each day of the week has its own card—signed with expressions of love from Robert. One card says, "She liked imaginary men best of all." Inside he wrote: "I'm sure this is true sometimes, but I'll try to be more like what you imagine." Yes, I remember. This was an exercise our marriage counselor had given him. At the time I was grateful for any proof of Robert's affection even if it was dictated by our therapist.

The truth of our marriage, it suddenly occurs to me, was revealed in this card: Robert was aware I might prefer an imaginary version of him to the man I dealt with every day. But this same therapist earlier had given Robert a different assignment: to do one act of thoughtfulness for me every day. That began an extended ritual of Robert bringing me tea in bed every morning. It was something that endured for years, and in that small gesture, Robert was the man I imagined.

"Namaste." My inscription to Robert in a birthday card dated July 26, 2008. "The divine in me salutes the divine in you." I wrote, "My birthday resolution to you is to find the divine in you each and every day and to honor it with peace, love, and serenity." In the emotional chaos that frequented our lives together I often turned to yoga. I read this card and see that it echoes the card that Robert gave me about my imagining him differently. I also see the date and know that three months later, after the full effect of the financial crisis in the fall of 2008 had been revealed, my resolution to see the divine in Robert had been shredded as completely as our bank accounts.

I turn my attention back to Robert's desk. He too has saved photos of the kids taken in grade school, all toothy grins and weird mom-styled haircuts. I rifle through the files. Some I'm familiar with as executor of his estate: I had gone through them in the year following his death. But then I was looking mostly for financials. I leaf through a folder that holds postcards from me; memorabilia from his travels; a calling card for Antoine's Restaurant in New Orleans; a letter from his ex-wife that appears to have been hand-delivered as it is addressed simply to Robert, but it also appears to never have been opened. Should I open it? I decide against it, in part because my own history with Robert is enough to excavate.

In the years since my divorce from Robert, and his death, my memories had taken on a sheen of calm. Now the narrative of the loving ex-wife caring for her former husband on his deathbed is being jostled as I dig into boxes of paper and reread old emails. I'd forgotten, or minimized, the disagreements we continued to have, the ongoing spats about money as Robert had to pay me alimony, childcare, and home maintenance on a home he was no longer living in. The bickering about timely payments. The pleas from Robert for forbearance.

Then this email exchange with Robert, while we were still living together and in the process of mediating our divorce: "Tara, I do accept responsibility for not being nice and I also accept responsibility for not living up to your expectations. I'm really sorry that I couldn't have been a better husband to you, and I think the reasons for that are many and complex, and I also don't think it would help your future to really try and figure them out. Perhaps, it will help me but that isn't the point. I promise to treat you with care, respect, and kindness as we move forward. Love, Robert."

Maybe not everyone has secrets, but probably most of us have things we tucked away in a drawer for a reason. I wonder if at any point after Robert was diagnosed he thought to himself, "I should go through those papers. I should throw out that file." If he thought it, he didn't do it. In his desk is a file folder with a large manilla envelope marked *Personal*. In it are evaluation sheets he'd written during one of his stays in rehab at Caron. Just reading them I felt I was invading his privacy. Lists of petty grievances and resentments. Heartbreaking feelings of self-loathing. The conflicts in our marriage. Unspoken animosities toward good friends. The unvarnished Robert. The feelings that tainted so many of his thoughts and interactions. What I experienced as ugliness, I could now see as unexpressed doubt, pain, and fear. Shouldn't Robert's demons die with him? My first thought was I should destroy the file. My second thought was, who am I to decide what should or should not be shared? Secrets undermine any chance of being honest with yourself. Keeping secrets creates shame, and shame is unconsciously passed on to the next generation.

The part of me that spent the decades of our marriage trying to know and understand Robert reads what he wrote with a mixture of alarm and recognition that this was the fuel behind so much of his behavior. While Robert may have been able to access some uncomfortable truths, it began and ended there. His answers were short—one or two words, a sentence or two if he was being expansive. Of course, I don't know what more Robert revealed when these worksheets were used as an entry point in one-on-one or group therapy. I do know that he didn't share any of this with me when he came home.

In many ways Robert's recovery was largely on the surface and didn't include me. He didn't drink, he went to meetings, he met AA friends for coffee every morning; his sobriety was something I silently monitored but was essentially excluded from. Robert had eight years of sobriety when he died, but it rarely felt to me that he was in recovery. AA is a twelve-step program that takes the alcoholic from Step One—admitting one is powerless over alcohol, through a progression of the steps that leads to a complete transformation of the flawed self into a person who feels, thinks, and behaves with awareness, love, and gratitude. Step Nine requires the recovering alcoholic to make amends to all those they have harmed. Robert never did Step Nine with me. I would have been an obvious place to start. He was to the end unwilling to be known or seen.

I'm still grappling with this. Maybe Robert didn't feel safe enough with me to reveal his sensitive truths. By the time he started recovery, our patterns of behavior were cemented by the roles established early in our marriage. I was the first mate, the one who "winched that line." Robert was the captain. The one who set the course. That gave him the space to claim autonomy in doing things that pleased only him, but it must also have left him lonely. You can't be Me and We at the same time.

Robert deeply wanted to be a beloved Captain, whatever the circumstances. During the course of our marriage, I saw him too often as Ahab, tyrannical and bent on his own mission, which the crew must accept without comment. But if he was Ahab, I was the first mate always threatening mutiny. And I could be fierce when I felt it was my duty to defend a position.

Once when I was out to dinner with Jack, he told me, "Mom, you can be scary." I laughed in surprise.

"Really?" I asked. Inwardly I took it as a compliment. I was fine with occasionally intimidating my teenage son into good behavior, but I didn't want intimidation to be how I held sway over Robert. And yet Robert required far more coercion to behave than our children ever did. And that perhaps was the crux of the problem. I wanted him to behave like an adult. No, I wanted him to *be* an adult. Robert saw this as my trying to control him.

Throughout our marriage, we participated in a classic push-pull power play. Who would control the money, the division of labor, the major life decisions? Whose priorities would come first? His? Mine? Our family's? These are not novel issues in a marriage, but they were constant and wearying in that constancy. For every agreement made, there was one broken. For every negotiation that resulted in a compromise, it was destined to be replayed. We never embraced what we learned. Every situation was the same Sisyphean struggle.

Often in the heat of an argument, Robert would snap at me, "I haven't changed!" He meant he was the same person I'd met and married—nothing about *him* was different. Even as it infuriated me, it made me laugh. I would say, "That's the problem, Robert. You haven't changed."

In fact, Robert did change. Not within the confines of the marriage, but in our more enduring relationship. Soon after our divorce was final Robert was thinking about buying a small house in town. He was living over the restaurant, which suited him temporarily, but he wanted a place where McCullough and Jack could come and stay. As I was still living in our family home a couple of miles up the road, it wasn't an immediate concern, but he was anticipating the sale of that house and he wanted to have a home where they would be comfortable. He'd found three houses he wanted to look at and asked me to come with him. He wanted to discuss them with me. After years of rebuffing my opinion, now he was seeking it out.

And not just about housing. Robert invited me to lunch about a month after the divorce was final. We sat at an outdoor café in town. As we ordered I wondered what was on his mind: was some part of the divorce settlement nagging at him, or had something happened with Jack or McCullough that he wanted to share with me? I thought, maybe all his friends were off doing other things, and he just wanted someone to eat with.

He started talking about Susan, the woman he was dating. Then he told me about a photographer who lived in Boston that he'd met and had dinner with, in Stockbridge, and about another woman he was conversing with online. He wanted to talk about his dating life. He wanted feedback, and he felt he could be his unvarnished self with me.

Fog was often a metaphor for our marriage as we blundered our way along, but now it took on a different light. The signposts were no longer black and white. We were in a wonderful grey area, obscuring the boundaries of how marriage and divorce are defined. We were navigating a new relationship as we went.

Robert would have told this story very differently. In fact, he wouldn't tell the story at all. I am the one who seeks explanations, who wants to revisit and examine incidents with the benefit of hindsight. As much as we disagreed, we also shared so much. In telling our story, I've had to decide what to keep and what to let go. Each of those decisions has created a new story: the story of a marriage, a family, a death, and the life that went on after that death.

As we came together again, in the last days of his life, neither of us spoke about our past. We did not revisit good or bad memories. There was no discussion of the future. We existed in the quiet of the moment. The fact of his coming back home, of being surrounded by his family, the ease of it, the abundance of peace, was the truth behind our story. His return gave me the opportunity to be the person I always wanted to be with him, and I gave him the gift of days filled with loving people keeping him company till his end.

ACKNOWLEDGMENTS

I am forever grateful to Walter Robinson, editor, friend, champion, without whom this book would not exist; and to my brother Brian, who from the beginning read every draft, and brought poetry and probing questions to every chapter.

Special thanks to Susan Cheever, whom I was lucky enough to have as my first-term advisor at Bennington, and to my singularly talented Bennington classmates for their support and encouragement.

I benefited enormously from friends who were willing to read my manuscript and offer their critiques as I sought to make sense of my marriage on the page. I'd particularly like to thank Sally D'Arcy, Susie Clarke, Nancy Henze, Cynthia Hochswender, Jamie Marshall, Jack O'Connell, Clint Smullyan, and Corina Zappia.

Huge appreciation to Susan Cheever, Michael Korda, and Joanne Proulx.

How can I properly thank all my family and friends who listened patiently as I endlessly processed my life before sitting down to write. You have been unfailing in your support of me, and I am indebted to each of you.

Thank you to the editors of *Cutleaf* for publishing my first chapter and inspiring me to continue.

And to Rodney Paterson, who shows me every day what it is to be loved.